MANAGING CHANGE

A How-To-Do-It Manual for Planning, Implementing, and Evaluating Change in Libraries

D0989071

182472

MANAGING CHANGE

A How-To-Do-It Manual for Planning, Implementing, and Evaluating Change in Libraries

SUSAN C. CURZON

REMOVED FROM THE
ALVERNO COLLEGE LIBRARY

*HOW-TO-DO-IT MANUALS
FOR LIBRARIES*
Number 2

Series Editor: Bill Katz

025.1
C983

NEAL-SCHUMAN PUBLISHERS, INC.
New York, London   1989

Alverno College
Library Media Center
Milwaukee, Wisconsin

Published by Neal-Schuman Publishers, Inc.
23 Leonard Street
New York, NY 10013

Copyright © 1989 by Susan C. Curzon

All rights reserved. Reproduction of this book, in whole or in part, without written permission of the publisher is prohibited.

Printed and bound in the United States of America

Library of Congress Cataloging-in-Publication Data

Curzon, Susan Carol.
    Managing change.

    (How to do it manuals for libraries ; no. 2)
    Includes index.
    1. Library planning.   2. Library administration.
3. Library personnel management.   4. Organizational
change—Management.   5. Library science—Technological
innovations—Management.   I. Title.   II. Series.
Z679.5.C87 1989   025.1   88-31409
ISBN 1-5557-0032-2

TO TERRY M. CURZON

CONTENTS

ACKNOWLEDGMENTS

I would like to thank the following people for their contribution to this book: Peter J. Curzon and Dr. James J. Sheridan for their generous assistance in reviewing the text. Dr. Robert H. Simmons who first helped me to demystify the change process. Professor Alberto Guerreiro Ramos whose belief in ethical management greatly influenced me. Arlene Schwartz who introduced me to my publisher, Patricia Glass Schuman. Gloria Carbajal who painstakingly typed the text. And to my colleagues in the Los Angeles County Public Library for their years of support and friendship.

SERIES EDITOR'S PREFACE

Change is everywhere in today's library environment. And so it is appropriate that *Managing Change* is one of the first in Neal-Schuman's series of "How-To-Do-It Manuals for Libraries." These books are user-oriented and issue-focused. They provide the answers librarians need to problems they face everyday.

Here is a practical text about change that neither berates nor punishes the reader. It is a straightforward guide to the benefits of change. Take time to read it carefully. The author is as constant in her effort for clarity as she is in her courtesy towards those who may not appreciate forward movement.

Anyone who has governed admits that administration is an art. Unlike some other arts, it can be mastered when one is willing to add anxious prayer to experience and a fair amount of luck.

Another approach is to listen to the experts. Dr. Curzon is one of those practical leaders whose gentle but firm persuasion is convincing and rewarding.

Not unexpectedly, the author approves of change, particularly at the library. At the same time, she understands human nature and the precious delight of standing quite still. In fact, she has a chapter on persuading the most conservative that a bit of movement can be beneficial. Significantly, she not only appreciates the reluctance of some to follow the management polestar, but equally understands the individual all too anxious to rush forward. Transformation, as she emphasizes, is a slow process. It has as many dangers as standing still. Throughout her work she evinces her conviction that working for an improved library is an achievable dream.

One may accept or disdain the discipline of administrative change, yet one cannot ignore it. When I went to library school, about the only real movement was in a new method of handling labels on the back of books. Oh, yes, and someone was mumbling about photocopying. Transformation was frowned upon, for what was good enough for Melvil was unalterable. Management techniques, IBM, television, and the ceremonial moves into the future changed all that. Today, even the casual observer realizes what online, CD-ROM, fax, and other new technologies have done to the quiet of the library.

The author has monitored the situation and handled it nicely. Her basic premise is that people are neither machines, nor ever meant to be machines. They require respect and attention—and just how much is evident in each of her chapters. One may take exception to this or that summary or technique, but not to the underlying policy, which is to admit to the pressures of a changing reality. Once that admission is made, it is reasonable to expect the prophet to come forward with a map of how to reach the goals dictated by the unsettled, even unsteady, winds of change.

And she does, guiding the reader step-by-step along the route. It is supremely important that each of the movements be integrated into the whole, and she accomplishes this with skill and appropriate explanation. Her task is especially difficult since it involves the art of dealing with goals still to be realized. How, for example, does one present the need for doing an about-face in administration, or at least veering slightly more to the right or the left? How does one make a decision within a group? How does one summon the courage to evaluate, and sometimes to admit error? Having detailed answers to these and scores of other related questions separate the true administrator from the amateur.

It is a happy thing to report that even the most inexperienced of administrators can learn how to become a captain, possibly even an admiral, on the good ship library by reading this book carefully. And this manual allows constant re-reading, if only to check on how to move an effort forward when it is stalled.

How many management guides have you read that are filled with giddy generalizations? This is a sober and thoughtful departure from the usual. First, it deals with change in libraries, not simply with how to move from Point Y to Point X in a billion-dollar international conglomerate. The fact that the guide is directed to professional librarians is a major plus. Second, drawing from a wealth of experience and common sense, the author offers an argument rooted in logic. Matters move so smoothly from sequence to sequence that anyone can grasp what to do next.

I am not sure who said preach not because you have to say something, but because you have something to say, but whoever said it would be happy with this guide. Dr. Curzon has given us a great guide to administration and, more important, to understanding one another and the world about us, which simply refuses to stand still. It may be just one damned thing after the other, but anyone who has a rendezvous with more than him- or herself will profit from reading this manual.

Bill Katz

INTRODUCTION

Twentieth-century librarianship has witnessed significant change in the last 40 years. The variety of services and formats provided, the professionalism of the profession, and the automation of many processes are some of the modern developments that affect the daily lives of library and information managers. But changes within librarianship are not the only significant changes. Improvements in world-wide communication and publishing, as well as the development of large databases, have evoked international interest in the gathering and dissemination of information. This global information network creates a complex and intense dimension for librarians unknown to their predecessors. The amount, diversity, and speed of information available through state-of-the-art technology has surrounded library managers with a continual flow of new directions and opportunities. Today, the manager of even the smallest library or agency faces what may seem an insurmountable task of managing constant change in the library and information environment.

Manage change, however, we must. Change that is out of control or mismanaged can prove destructive to any organization. A knowledgeable approach to the management of change enables library and information administrators to retain the long-range vision of their organization, to make choices about costly technological and facility investments, and to secure a permanent place as one of society's major information providers. In addition, a skilled manager can reduce or eliminate the sometimes devastating impact that organizational change can have on individuals.

To manage change effectively summons all the talents and abilities of a manager. Change is difficult, complex, and ambiguous. On the one hand, change, and the growth and experience it brings, can be very beneficial. On the other hand, people are habituated to a pattern of behaving and resist when threatened with a change. Moreover, people's abilities to adapt to change varies considerably not only from person to person, but also from situation to situation. Unpredictability is a fundamental part of people's response to change. It is ironic that when people are stable and secure, they yearn for change. When people have too much change, they yearn for stability.

The challenge for managers, therefore, is how to control and implement change. We know from past experience how chaotic change can be. We know how quickly it gets out of control and forms a life of its own. Many managers looking down the well-traveled road of change see only the magnitude of effort and the certainty of disruption. Many are deterred at this point, reluctant to encounter the inevitable confusion and upset. However, by understanding the process of change and by shifting our perspective and approach, we can significantly reduce negative experiences and improve the chance of successful change.

For the purposes of effective management, change should be viewed as a logical stream. This attitude enables a manager to perform at an executive level, controlling and guiding the process to the desired end. While every experienced manager knows that it is rare for an organizational process to proceed smoothly, a manager who has penetrated the logic of change has the advantage of seeing through the problems to the next step. A library manager without this long-distance vision may become immersed in the confusion that change can bring or intimidated by the feelings that change can unleash. The primary meaning of the word "manage" is "to succeed in accomplishing." It presumes the ability to control the situation and to avoid the process of the organization controlling the manager. Management of change cannot be done haphazardly. A manager must keep to a steady course, anticipate the next step.

As precipitous and confusing as change can be, it has a logic that can be captured, modified, and developed. *Managing Change* is a guidebook that will enable library administrators to prepare for and manage change within any type of library or information agency. It will take the manager through each of the successive phases of managing change.

When change is viewed logically, it can be divided into a sequence of events. This sequence takes the manager from the point of preparing the organization for change to the point of evaluating how successful the change has been. This sequence should be used in the management of any change.

CONCEPTUALIZING: envisioning the change.

PREPARING: readying the organization for change.

ORGANIZING THE PLANNING GROUP: gathering people to plan the change.

PLANNING: creating systems and allocating resources to effect the change.

DECIDING: the decision-making process.

MANAGING THE INDIVIDUAL: introducing the changes to staff.

CONTROLLING RESISTANCE: management of staff who resist change.

IMPLEMENTING: creating acceptance of change within the organization.

EVALUATING: assessing the value of the change.

These phases are progressive and should not be overlooked or neglected even if speed is paramount. Attention must be given to each phase or the probability of the project disintegrating is high. Change is inevitable in organizations. Although a part of each one of us wants to keep things as they are, we all recognize how fundamentally change is a part of life. Organizations today are no longer in a solid state, that is, no longer stable for extended periods of time. The most we can expect are temporary lulls between changes.

Once this reality is accepted, every good library and information manager must strive for a coherent approach to the management of change. By examining the organizational processes that will affect and be affected by change and by understanding the impact of change upon individuals, managers can prepare themselves to handle change effectively.

OVERVIEW

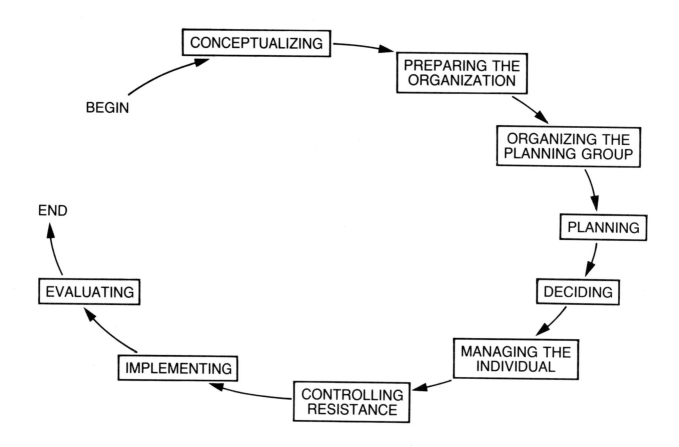

1 CONCEPTUALIZING

STEP 1
Develop awareness

STEP 2
Understand the change

STEP 3
Decide on the change

STEP 4
Envision the change

2 PREPARING THE ORGANIZATION

STEP 1
Listen to staff

STEP 2
Respect staff

STEP 3
Maintain a healthy balance between task and people

STEP 4
Be fair with everyone

STEP 5
Be supportive

STEP 6
Be committed

STEP 7
Be trustworthy and open

STEP 8
Be credible

STEP 9
Be collegial

3 ORGANIZING THE PLANNING GROUP

STEP 1
Assemble the planning group

STEP 2
Set parameters

STEP 3
Build a team

STEP 4
Plan the first meeting

4 PLANNING

STEP 1
Develop the vision

STEP 2
Create options

STEP 3
Evaluate options

STEP 4
Choose an option

STEP 5
Write the goals and objectives

STEP 6
Develop the plan

5 DECIDING

STEP 1
Review all documents

STEP 2
Evaluate the pros and cons

STEP 3
Consider the consequences

STEP 4
Allow for mature deliberation

STEP 5
Avoid barriers

STEP 6
Make the right decisions

6 MANAGING THE INDIVIDUAL

STEP 1
Prepare for the meeting

STEP 2
Discuss the change

STEP 3
Keep the channels of communication open

STEP 4
Monitor performance

7 CONTROLLING RESISTANCE

STEP 1
Identify the techniques of resistance

STEP 2
Analyze the source of resistance

STEP 3
Counteract resistance

8 IMPLEMENTING

STEP 1
Appoint a transition manager

STEP 2
Choose the right timing

STEP 3
Formally introduce the change

STEP 4
Pilot the change

STEP 5
Avoid change disintegration

STEP 6
Follow-through with the change

STEP 7
Release the trappings of change

9 EVALUATING

STEP 1
Choose the time for the evaluation

STEP 2
Appoint the evaluators

STEP 3
Re-examine the goals

STEP 4
Choose the method of evaluation

STEP 5
Identify the problems

STEP 6
Avoid roadblocks

STEP 7
Make needed adjustments

STEP 8
Review the change process

STEP 9
Share the information

1 CONCEPTUALIZING

STEP 1
Develop awareness

STEP 2
Understand the change

STEP 3
Decide on the change

STEP 4
Envision the change

Conceptualizing, the first and most critical of all the phases, enables the manager to assess the nature and desirability of the change and to envision its direction. The introduction of change into an organization is not a matter to be taken lightly. Even a change that appears small to an executive can play havoc with staff morale and management credibility.

The period of conceptualization allows a manager the opportunity to consider what change is necessary, why it should occur, and what converging or conflicting forces may affect it. This is the phase in which leadership is most evident as the manager sets directions and examines alternatives and consequences. It is imperative that a manager think deeply about change. Time invested in comprehending the nature of change, checking it against established patterns, and envisioning what direction it will take can relieve the organization of considerable aggravation later on. Rushing to planning and implementation is foolhardy. The larger the scope of a change, the more risky any haste will be. But do not underestimate a minor change, either.

A word of caution. In the best of situations, conceptual thought should regularly occupy a percentage of a library manager's time. The lack of adequate staffing levels, the constant flow of library patrons, and the presumption that work must be tangible to be worthwhile frequently prevent the manager from setting aside time just for thought. Therefore, unless this allocation of time is an established practice, particular care must be given to create such periods or this phase will be lost in the pressure of day-to-day work. So critical is this phase that no change should proceed without it. After all, how can a good manager send staff on a journey when the path is not known?

While conceptualization does require depth of thought, the process itself is quite straightforward and can be broken into four steps, which will supply the manager with all the structure necessary to conceptualize.

STEP 1
Develop awareness

Change always begins with a manager's awareness that change is needed. Such awareness can be sudden, such as a budget cut or a dramatic drop in circulation, but it usually makes a subtler appearance. A recurring problem, a patron complaint, a brief mention of an idea at a staff meeting may make the manager aware that change is necessary in the organization. It is critical that the manager be able to identify the source of the change. By knowing the source, the manager can determine what amount of control can be exercised over the change. Change can come from many different sources. It can be externally motivated, internally motivated, or a combination of both: it can be imposed upon the organization or initiated by the organization. Let's look at each one.

External Change: External forces of change are usually social, political, economic, or technological. The development of a large minority population on a campus is a social change. The election of a conservative library board in place of a liberal board is a political change. A budget decrease is an economic change. The development of laser discs is a technological change. These changes are externally generated, but may dramatically affect library service and be very difficult to control.

Internal Change: Internal forces can also bring about change. For example, a work unit within the library may have emerged in public services that would be better suited to technical services, or a manager may want to automate the book order process or charge fees for a particular service. The advantage of internally motivated change is that it is usually positive. It would be rare, and rash, for a manager to bring negative change to an organization. Managers are, by the nature of their position, interested in the success of the organization. Negative change would damage that primary purpose.

Combined Forces of Change: More often than not, change is a combination of external and internal forces. Libraries are subject to all the demands and pressures of society. The external development of a new technology may spark an internal movement to accept the new technology and lead to a process such as circulating videocassettes. Libraries seeking new ways to automate a procedure could inspire the private sector to develop an attractive system. It is important to remember that change does not occur in a vacuum; it depends on many forces and ideas.

Imposed Change: What about change that is imposed upon the organization? Very few libraries have no parent entity. Governments and corporations can and do create pressures and control the budgets of libraries. Such influences often impose changes that even the most skillful manager cannot avoid. For a library manager, imposed change is always external. For middle managers, imposed change may be from the library director. If the change is inevitable, it is important not to resist to it. Better instead to manage it successfully.

Initiated Change: The best change is initiated from within. Here the managers and staff can select the changes they think will enhance the well-being of the library. Of course, caution is still needed because any change can go awry, but the chances of success are greatly enhanced. One note here. Sometimes managers are too precipitous; they announce a change to their bosses before fully thinking it through. This does not mean that managers should withhold ideas from their supervisors. It only means that caution should be exercised. If not, managers can find themselves with a board of trustees or a vice-president who likes the idea very much while the manager is having second thoughts. If early announcements seem desirable, then discuss the entire change sequence outlined.

An interesting part of managing change is that, whether the change is external or internal, imposed or initiated, the process remains the same. It might be intensified or accelerated, depending upon the threat to the organization, but the sequence of phases is still necessary.

The awareness of change or a need for change, should be a trigger for the manager to begin the change sequence. It schools us to have realistic expectations about our ability to control change. If change is negative but within our control, a manager can move quickly to minimize its effect on the organization. If change is negative but not controllable, such as large political or financial shifts, a manager can manage reactions and the change's integration into the organization.

STEP 2
Develop understanding

Once change has made itself known in the organization, the manager's task is to understand the nature, pattern, and target of change. Grasping these elements will enable a manager to plan for the necessary depth and speed of the change process. By asking:

What is the nature of the change? Is it positive? Is it negative?
What is the pattern of change? Is it permanent? Periodic? Isolated?
What are the targets of change? Is it process? Structure? Technology? People?

A manager can unravel the complex threads that entangle change and gain a more realistic picture of the change if these questions are asked and effectively answered.

WHAT IS THE NATURE OF THE CHANGE?

Change can be either positive or negative. That is, it can have either a good or a bad influence on the library.

Positive: Positive change is anything that will be either immediately or ultimately beneficial to the library—for example, the influx of new monies, the approval of building plans, or the addition of new librarians. In these situations, most people will see the benefit and anticipate change gladly.

Negative: Negative change, of course, is anything that will be harmful to the library. A 35 percent budget cut, a fire or flood, or other structural damage are all examples of negative change. When change is negative, the planning will be, not different, but intensified. Negative change, apart from the damage it does to the processes and structure of an organization, brings out aggressive and hostile emotions. Intensity refers not only to the speed with which planning must be done, but to the thoroughness of the thinking required. All ramifications must be considered in order to minimize damage and forestall avoidable complications.

It is important to note that change is often ambiguous—neither clearly positive nor absolutely negative. For example, automation, which is generally good for libraries, often has many negative aspects as the staff adjusts to changes. Building a new library is usually good, but the process is frequently traumatic. Even adding new staff, which should be a source of joy, can raise conflicts about which units will get the help.

A skillful manager looks for the positive in the negative and the negative in the positive. If you are faced with the nightmare of a budget cut, use that unfortunate circumstance to examine priorities or to reaffirm commitments to certain services. Take that time to establish strong bonding between staff as everyone prepares for a threat to library services. Conversely, do not take positive change blithely. A manager may be thrilled to receive a new library, but what about staff who may be commuting longer distances, having their bus routes altered, or losing a window office? Nothing will be 100 percent one way or the other. Not everyone will always agree on whether a change is positive or negative. Therefore, a manager must ferret out the negative or positive influences in every change and make them work to the organization's advantage.

WHAT IS THE PATTERN OF CHANGE?

Many events in a library year are cyclical. There are periods of budget allocation preparation and review, equipment ordering, hiring of staff, and materials acquisitions. As work ebbs and flows in the organization, so does change. It is natural to think of change as an isolated occurrence. That actually is only one of three possible patterns. Change can be permanent, periodic, or isolated.

Permanent Change: Permanent change will be long-standing—a move to a new facility, for example. Change that is permanent needs the same intensity of planning that negative change needs. Obviously, if something has to be lived with for a long time, it makes sense to plan carefully. What is difficult is getting people to accept that the change is permanent. Much energy can be wasted fighting what cannot be changed.

Periodic Change: Budget cycles, changing forms of automation, or vacant staff positions are periodic problems. Some require fairly low-level planning, such as adjusting work schedules to cover vacancies. Some, such as upgrading an automated circulation system, require more planning. Nevertheless, it is important for a manager to convince employees that whatever change is made may be changed and changed again because of the recurring nature of the problem.

Isolated Change: A devastating fire or flood or substantial financial gifts are examples of isolated events that will bring change. Such changes require a one-time marshaling of the organization's energy. There are two problems associated with major change that is isolated. First, the organizational processes usually are not adequate to meet isolated change. Very few librarians, for example, really have a satisfactory plan for emergencies and must usually scramble to develop a plan while the emergency is occurring. Second, isolated change tends to become permanent.

Assessing the pattern of change enables the manager to consider how much to engage the library in the change process. Obviously, a change that is small and isolated will require a lot less effort than change that is large and permanent.

WHAT IS THE TARGET OF CHANGE:

All change has a target. There is always some part of the organization that will experience the primary impact. The target of change is that aspect that will be modified, developed, altered, or terminated in the change process.

There are four targets of change:

a process change
a structural change
a technological change
a people change

Process Change: A process change might be a new form for requisitioning supplies or a new procedure at the reference or circulation desk. Think about a process change as a change in the way that we do business.

Structural Change: A structural change refers to the organization of the library. Most libraries are organized into a hierarchical structure with a director at the top of the pyramid. If a unit or division were moved to report to a different supervisor, that would be a structural change.

Technological Change: Technological change is something about which libraries know a great deal. This, of course, refers to such developments as automating the circulation system, converting the catalog onto compact discs, or providing on-line reference. It tends to be a very complex change because technical expertise, as well as a knowledge of the management of change, is needed.

People Change: Sometimes people's behavior is the target of change. Perhaps there is an unfriendly attitude at the circulation desk or telephone etiquette is not quite what it should be.

Remember that people are affected in all changes. An organization may target people or their behavior as needing the most change, but there never is a time when processes, structure, or technology will not have an impact on people. Managers must never make the mistake of saying that the library is only changing a process or a new piece of equipment. Behind every typewriter, computer, and projector sits a person who will be affected by change.

Try not to target more than one type of change of any magnitude in any one year. It is not uncommon to have libraries plan for change in all four areas and then wonder why the staff is angry or under stress. Managers who are in control have a steady hand in integrating change into an organization.

Considering the nature, pattern, and target of change will help the library manager to understand where on the spectrum the change will fall. If it has been determined that the change is positive, internally motivated, and permanent, everyone can enjoy the process. If, on the other hand, the change is permanent, negative, and externally imposed, all the skills and talent of the staff will be called into play. While a manager cannot afford to be cavalier about any significant change in the organization, knowledge of the impact that the nature, target, and pattern of change will have helps in planning an appropriate strategy.

STEP 3
Decide on the change

The change process has various decision points. The first one—the decision to engage in the change process. Realizing that change is needed is one thing; deciding to change is quite another. Obviously, there are circumstances in which a manager does not have a choice, but if possible, assess the consequences of change before proceeding.

One of the characteristics of change is that it can appear more urgent and valuable than it really is. Change can be exciting, and while it is human nature to go toward that which is new and different, this does not necessarily make for sound organizational decisions.

In order to understand the consequences of change, ask these eight questions:

> Is the change legitimate?
> Is the change a priority?
> Is the change worth the price?
> What are the limits of the organization?
> What are the parameters of change?
> Is the change consistent with the organization?
> Is change needed?
> Has the organization as a whole been considered?

IS THE CHANGE LEGITIMATE?
Legitimate change is change that has been decided upon in a logical and rational fashion and that has taken the organization as a whole into account. Legitimate change should not subvert, or replace other processes in an organization. However, many managers use change to solve a problem that is best solved in another way. For example, it is not uncommon for there to be a reorganization or reclassification around a problem employee. The goal is to lower the person's position, change the reporting structure, or make the employee uncomfortable enough to quit. This is not legitimate change. The manager is avoiding confronting the employee about

poor performance. That employee should be sent into the disciplinary system, not the change system.

IS THE CHANGE A PRIORITY?

Change can be very attractive. Librarians like to be thought of as progressive. In fact, the professional literature bombards managers with the need to be up-to-date. Much of this is good, but it is not healthy for an organization to go after change for its own sake. While minor changes will occur almost daily, major changes must be weighed against the mission of the library and its annual goals. All change should be planned in conjunction with other goals and the capacity to deliver. Human resources must be considered. Managers must also be careful not to set priorities according only to their individual preferences for a project.

IS THE CHANGE WORTH THE PRICE?

Even good change will have a downside. Some change has such far-reaching side effects that it's not worth the price. For example, productivity drops as people learn a new system. If change has negative aspects, there will be dissent, anger, and alienation amongst the staff. Change that goes on too long results in boredom and lack of enthusiasm for implementation. A manager must consider carefully whether the benefits outweigh the costs and if the risks are worth it. If the benefits do not outweigh the costs, why proceed?

WHAT ARE THE LIMITS OF THE ORGANIZATION?

Is there a manager out there who really wants to reclassify 50 employees, change all the division heads, automate the circulation system, and open two new branches at the same time? Sometimes it is unavoidable that large projects will come together, but there is a point where the staff is stretched to the limit. There is a relationship between time and quality. Good work simply cannot be done if everything in the organization is a mad rush. When taking on projects that involve major change, consider how much flex time is available to fulfill the normal requirements of the organization as well as a major undertaking. Be sure to place in that analysis time for conceptual thought. This is particularly important as many library managers are working supervisors or operational managers, which means that they have a substantial body of work to do themselves besides directing the work of others.

WHAT ARE THE PARAMETERS OF CHANGE?

Change has a way of creeping up. Perhaps the project calls for automating fiscal services, but in the process of the study it becomes apparent that the supply order process could also benefit. Perhaps there is a crowded section on the first floor of the library, and suddenly everyone is talking about shifting all three floors. Since change affects relationships between parts of an organization, it can easily get out of control. Set clear parameters around what can and will be done. File good ideas away for next year. However, if it is apparent that a major change will ultimately be better than the minor one that was anticipated, do not proceed with the latter simply because the parameters were set for a minor change. The entire concept may have to be delayed until adequate planning is done.

IS THE CHANGE CONSISTENT WITH THE ORGANIZATION?

Each organization has its own culture. Some are traditional, some entrepreneurial, some formal, and some conservative. The culture is a manifestation of the values of an organization—that is, those concepts, such as education or freedom, that a society or body of people hold in high regard. For example, most librarians value learning, life-long education, freedom of information, and free library service. Such values must be understood and articulated before a change can occur. Values and culture in an organization control much of its direction and decision-making. Change that is not consistent with the prevailing culture is unlikely to be accepted. For example, if a library values free access to information, the staff will have a difficult time accepting a new, fee-based service. If the library has been traditionally accustomed to authoritative managers, a new manager who is participative in approach will cause confusion until the differences are understood.

It is quite possible that the values and culture of the organization will themselves be the target of change. One important reason to make values a target is that not all values are good. However, changing values requires considerable sophistication, as managers will usually share the values of the organization.

One of the major pitfalls of change is that it stirs up discussions of values. All organizations are driven by values, but most not consciously so. In a major change, particularly one with negative aspects, values will come to the fore. A manager must not be afraid to confront such issues, but must be aware of their power. Values that are overlapping or colliding can stall even the most dynamic of changes.

IS CHANGE NEEDED?

American society appreciates change. There are some people in every profession who are overly fond of change. These are not to be confused with visionaries, although they often are. They simply like change and like to get things stirred up. People who are overly attached to change generally do not understand its impact. A manager must make sure that change is really needed and is not being undertaken merely for its own sake.

HAS THE ORGANIZATION AS A WHOLE BEEN CONSIDERED?

No part of the organization exists in a vacuum. All parts are dependent upon each other. To change one thing in a library is to affect another. The consciousness of this is called a systems perspective. It simply means that the manager understands the flow of processes through an organization and the interdependency of each aspect. When planning for change, one needs to consider the organization as a whole. For example, if a body of work is being transferred, think about the sending and the receiving division. Will it affect deliveries, personnel, work spaces? Minor points can trip up the best of change.

Only after a library manager is clear on these aspects should a tentative decision be made to proceed. If the cost is too high, the project unwieldly, the resources minimal, a steady hand will be needed to defer or reject the change. Change needs to be stopped at this point before investing more heavily in the process.

STEP 4

Envision the change

By now, the manager should have considerable clarity about the change. The manager knows the source of the change, understands its nature, pattern, and target and has questioned its validity and motivation. The next step is to envision the change.

Envisioning is the final step in Conceptualizing. Conceptualizing refers to the process of thinking through the entire project. Envisioning refers specifically to developing a clear mental picture of what the change will be. Envisioning is so critical that no one should consider proceeding without completing this phase. For example, perhaps the manager has received numerous complaints about poor reference service. In this step, the manager would envision, or picture mentally, what the outcome of the change will be. The manager should be able to see clearly all the librarians at the reference desk delivering courteous, effective, and efficient service. In other words, here the manager develops an overall vision of the project.

Obviously, at this point, not every detail will be calculated and no goals will be developed. That work will come in Planning. Envisioning is the mental map, or set of instructions, that the manager will give to the planning group. Without a clear picture it would be very difficult to convey what is expected. It would be easy for the planning group to go off in a completely inappropriate direction. It is important to realize that the manager must think about what outcome is desired. This picture should be ideal. Reality will come soon enough.

Notice that this is a top-down management style—that is, the manager sets the directions. This does not mean that the planning group cannot re-shape the vision, but only that the manager has provided the necessary leadership.

Be careful not to be too formal at this point.

Depending upon the confidentiality of the issue, the manager can involve a couple of key thinkers to assist with this step and any other process in conceptualization. The product of a group is always better than the product of one. However, if the change is major and the library large enough to have a number of managers, consider having at least one manager remain uninvolved with the change. This person will have greater objectivity and can look out for trouble.

CONCLUSION

In Conceptualizing, we learned to think through where the change came from (awareness), what it is like (understanding), whether it is a good idea for the library (deciding), and what the product of change should be (envisioning). This phase forces us to think deeply about the change and not to accept it at face value. Introducing change into an organization is a serious matter. A superficial approach will minimize its success rate, but maximize its capacity to aggravate managers and staff alike. There is no substitute in management for clear, deep thinking on issues. The work of conceptualizing is never done, of course, but as a formal phase it now gives way to Preparing the Organization.

QUICK CHECK

STEP 1
Develop awareness

A. Is the change externally motivated?
B. Is the change internally motivated?
C. Is the change imposed?
D. Is the change initiated from within?

STEP 2
Develop understanding

A. What is the nature of the change?
   Is it positive?
   Is it negative?
B. What is the pattern of change?
   Is it permanent?
   Is it periodic?
   Is it isolated?
C. What is the target of change?
   Is it process?
   Is it structural?
   Is it technological?
   Is it people?

STEP 3
Decide on the change

A. Is the change legitimate?
B. Is the change a priority?
C. Is the change worth the price?
D. What are the limits of the organization?
E. What are the parameters of change?
F. Is the change consistent with the organization?
G. Is change needed?
H. Has the organization as a whole been considered?

STEP 4
Envision the change

A. What is the desired state?
B. Is an informal group needed?

2 PREPARING THE ORGANIZATION

What makes some libraries receptive to change and others resistant? Why are some employees enthusiastic about new developments while others are critical and fearful? Why can some managers gain ready acceptance of change while others meet with nothing but resentment?

The answer lies within the decision makers' management philosophy. There is a certain management style within organizations that creates an environment conducive to change. If this style, which we will discuss in depth in a moment, is not present, the probability of successful change is greatly reduced. This style can soften people's resistance to change and nurture those qualities that will enhance change. An organization lacking this management style will encounter substantially greater resistance to change.

Change cannot flourish in a rigid environment. Successful change needs openness, honest communication, and receptivity. If people are accustomed to being tightly supervised, having no authority, obeying all rules and regulations, and being criticized, they will not be free to offer the commitment and creativity upon which successful change relies. Managers prepare organizations for change through their own style. When managers exhibit characteristics conducive to change, the staff will respond in kind. Every manager should adopt the following steps to prepare the organization for change.

STEP 1
Listen to staff

Listening is one of the most fundamental ways to demonstrate respect for another individual and one of the most powerful ways to build self-esteem. Having another person's complete attention and interest is a rewarding experience.

All people are sometimes guilty of being poor listeners. Listening is a very active process, not the passive one it is often assumed to be. It requires energy to listen attentively to what another person is saying. It also requires energy to shut off internal conversations that keep people busy judging, thinking ahead to what they want to say, or daydreaming. Managers should learn to be good listeners, to really perceive both the words and the body language of the other person.

Sometimes, though, the higher managers go, the less they listen. Actually, the higher managers go, the more they should listen. How many of us, while hearing an employee problem have looked at watches, fiddled with phone messages, or thought ahead to the ten next things on our agendas. The employee knows this and resents it. If listening skills are bad enough, people will begin to feel rebuffed and will eventually cease to communicate all but the most necessary items. Valuable communication about feelings, goals, and problems will go unsaid. An employee who cannot communicate with a boss eventually becomes alienated. A boss who does not communicate with the staff becomes isolated. Both are extreme results of the inability to listen correctly.

Obviously, good communication is vital in a change process. Change brings many new feelings and creates new problems. If people are not already effective communicators, the communication process will be even more hampered by the additional stress placed upon it. Learn to listen well and place a priority on good listening in the organization.

STEP 2
Respect staff

Respect means to hold in esteem another person's self worth. What does it mean when managers say, "We have respect for our staff?" Do we as managers take the time for individuals? Do we really feel that each person makes a contribution? Do we think that everyone is special? Do we credit people with good judgment? Do we recognize good work?

Or does everyone think they are a cog in the wheel? Do we think that people only have good judgment according to their level in the hierarchy? Do we criticize the flaws in work before we praise the effort? Do we casually override people's schedules and appointments to meet our own needs? Do we neglect to say "hello" or "good morning" or observe common courtesies to everyone on the staff?

Respect begins with a sincere recognition of each person's value. When people are accustomed to being treated with respect at all levels, then the same decent behavior will accompany change. Think how much more pleasant an internal environment the library will have when everyone is certain of being dealt with in a respectful manner. These courtesies will ripple outward. Remember, without the support of staff, no manager is effective.

STEP 3
Maintain a healthy balance between task and people

A library manager has a dual responsibility, for tasks and for people. The tasks must be accomplished so the library may fulfill its mission, but the well-being of staff must always be of equal concern. Sometimes these two responsibilities seem mutually exclusive, but attention to tasks and attention to people are both essential. Now, it is possible that not every project or event will permit perfect equality but it should be obvious to all that if one or the other has priority, it is only a temporary response to a special, limited situation. A chronic complaint about staff today is lack of loyalty towards organizations. Is it any wonder? Layoffs and poor reorganizations communicate to staff that the organization is not loyal to them. Why should they return loyalty?

All experienced managers know that loyalty is a false god. It is only natural for people to be looking out for their own interest, even though they may be very concerned with the welfare of the organization. However, our management ethics require us to build humane organizations. Therefore, regardless of the loyalty that we do or do not receive, we still take people's needs into account even as we accomplish the tasks. As it turns out, managers will gain a great deal of support from staff by paying attention to all parts of an organization. This support will be critical during periods of change when it is most common for people to become victims of the process.

STEP 4
Be fair with everyone

Everyone knows that there is no such thing as absolute fairness, yet it remains of paramount importance to us. When people have not been fairly dealt with, they feel cheated and resentful. Even though there are sometimes good reasons for not being completely fair, managers should strive to be as fair as possible. Favoritism or personal prejudices should not be the source of decisions. Fairness also means consistency. A decision for one should be a decision for all unless there is a substantial reason for exceptions. People who know they will receive fair treatment will demonstrate much less resistance to change, particularly in personnel matters.

STEP 5
Be supportive

An organization full of people can be a surprisingly lonely place. Rare is the organization where people rush to help another with a problem, support each other in difficult situations, and volunteer to assist each other with a complex project or a work overload. In such an organization, the environment would be charged with teamwork, cooperation, and positive directions.

Being supportive is an often overlooked but vital aspect of change. Staff who support their boss, bosses who back up their staff, managers who support each other's initiatives create a wholesome and cushioning environment for change. The threatening aspects of change are greatly reduced by people ready to help other people.

To achieve supportive behavior, be supportive and talk supportively. A band of supportive people can have far-reaching effects on the well-being of the organization. A manager should emphasize, model, and reward supportive behavior.

STEP 6
Be committed

Change of any magnitude requires more than a passing effort. Managers must be determined to bring about the successful completion of the project. Commitment calls for managers to take responsibility for what is occurring and to take such independent action as may be needed.

Managers must encourage staff to be consistently conscientious in taking care of any aspects that will improve the change, without always waiting for specific directions. In successful change, everyone shoulders the responsibility. This will make the workload easier for all and will substantially increase the quality of the outcome.

Moreover, commitment generally brings a great deal of positive thought toward any change. People who are committed to a goal are determined people. Determined people will overcome barriers and roadblocks to successful change.

STEP 7
Be trustworthy and open

Trust is earned by the honesty of our actions. Managers must make every attempt to speak truthfully in all matters to the staff and encourage staff to speak truthfully in turn. When managing a change project, good decision-making is absolutely dependent upon the accuracy of information. If some information is not getting through, the decision, and ultimately the change, could be skewed.

Of course, managers cannot always be completely open. Confidentiality, as it pertains to many personnel or union issues, will prohibit complete free-speaking. It is better in situations such as this to tell staff that the issue is confidential. They might not like it, but will appreciate it far more than a falsehood or cover-up.

Trust will become critical if the change will affect jobs and positions. Since this is particularly threatening, both managers and staff should have a good history of trust behind them before attempting such changes.

STEP 8
Be credible

Credibility simply means that a person inspires belief. Unfortunately, there is sometimes an adversarial relationship between managers and staff. Occasionally, there is good cause for it, but more often than not it is in the nature of the relationship itself. It is all too common that employees do not believe what managers say or are convinced that most managers will pull something given half a chance. The peculiarity of this attitude is that it is more general than specific. Many staff members will like or feel close to their boss, but will still talk about what management is "up to" in a general and impersonal way. This stems from seeing the organization as an impersonal entity rather than as a network of people.

During change, a great deal of stress is placed on both the organization and the individual. It is said that the true character of an individual is only revealed in adverse situations. Likewise, staff members may reveal their worst suspicions, or their truest feelings about management, under the stressful conditions that change brings. But, if the manager's credibility is firmly established, the staff will sustain their confidence even in difficult situations.

Managers must be committed to doing what they say they will do. Remember that words without action have no meaning. When there is a substantial difference between what is said and what occurs, staff has the right to call management credibility into question.

On the other hand, managers must help staff to see that it is not always possible to bring certain things to pass. Managers may have had good plans, but circumstances may have prevented carrying out the work. It does staff members no justice to permit them to be naive about the pressures that can counteract the best of intentions.

In addition, when a manager makes a decision that is not understood, the staff needs to learn how to give that manager the benefit of the doubt. We are all very quick to judge and to condemn another's actions without understanding the full story. These quick judgments can cause a great deal of conflict. Management credibility is established in two ways—first, by managers whose words can be believed; second, by staff and peers willing to withhold judgment until the reasons behind a decision can be fully communicated.

STEP 9
Be collegial

Librarians, through their long years in school, have a special affinity for a collegial atmosphere. On paper, one manager may be the boss, but professionally, librarians are equal. The concept of "primus inter pares" or "first among equals" is particularly effective with librarians. The establishment of collegiality encourages teamwork. If people feel respected for their education and judgment and are allowed to develop good working relationships with each other, they will provide a comfortable haven for change. Many times rivalry occurs in organizations when one group feels another does not understand it or seeks power over it. In a collegial environment, where there are strong networks and relationships, it is more difficult for adversarial relationships to bloom. People with strong relationships will work well together and will work out differences for the sake of the relationships. These are key ingredients for successful change. Many problems that loom large for an unfriendly group will be solved by a group with a good working history. The manager should set the tone for collegial behavior in the library.

CONCLUSION

The most difficult part of preparing the organization for change is for managers to honestly assess their own management style. This requires a high degree of self-awareness as well as an articulated management philosophy. Modern managers do not have the luxury of allowing their management style to flow from their personality alone, or as a reaction to events. All management styles need a rational basis.

If the manager is concerned that very few of the characteristics outlined above are held by fellow managers and staff and wants those characteristics widely shared, the manager should consider the development of such characteristics as a change project. All organizations have their own unique culture. To change the culture of an entire organization is a difficult project and should be managed according to the change sequence outlined in this book.

A manager who wants to bring about successful change in the organization must be attentive to the nine steps in this chapter.

With these steps, the library manager can create a more open organization, that is, an organization whose staff is flexible, honest, supportive, and committed. The more open an organization is, the more capable it is weathering change. An open organization is not an invitation to chaos. The manager still exerts control and exercises authority. However, staff and managers alike are more involved in a partnership that sees the success of the enterprise as rewarding to all. Open organizations are safe, humane places: because people are at ease, they are also places that demonstrate less rigidity and resistance to change. Build an open organization for the effective management of change.

QUICK CHECK

STEP 1
Listen to staff

A. Do managers give people full attention when listening?
B. Do managers listen well no matter what position they hold?

STEP 2
Respect staff

A. Do managers take time for people?
B. Do managers observe regular courtesies?

STEP 3
Maintain a healthy balance between task and people

A. Are tasks and people considered equally?
B. Do managers demonstrate loyalty to staff?

STEP 4
Be fair with everyone

A. Do the managers strive to be impartial in decisions?
B. Are managers consistent in their decisions?

STEP 5
Be supportive

A. Does the staff help each other out?
B. Are cooperation and support emphasized and rewarded?

STEP 6
Be committed

A. Do people act independently?
B. Do people take responsibility for the work?

STEP 7
Be trustworthy and open

A. Are the managers honest in sharing information?
B. Do the managers indicate when information is confidential?

STEP 8
Be credible

A. Are the managers' words and actions consistent?
B. Does the staff wait for the manager to explain the decision before making judgments?

STEP 9
Be collegial

A. Do people feel respected for their education and judgment?
B. Do people feel like a "body of professionals"?

3 ORGANIZING THE PLANNING GROUP

STEP 1
Assemble the planning group

STEP 2
Set parameters

STEP 3
Build a team

STEP 4
Plan the first meeting

For all but the most minor changes, a capable planning group must be organized. Generally speaking, change, particularly change of any magnitude, is best done by a group. Time and time again, studies have shown that the work product of a group is superior to the work product of one person. When a group is working well together, its creative power and problem-solving ability is considerable. It is to the manager's advantage to pull together the best planning group possible to design the change.

One of management's greatest sins is the casual way groups are pulled together. Half the time, managers are happy to get anyone to volunteer. Such an approach will not work in the management of change as it is the correct group, not just any group, that will determine the project's success.

Organizing a group to plan the change calls for structure and strategy. Working through the following four steps will help the manager organize the planning group into an effective work force.

STEP 1
Assemble the planning group

A manager must think strategically before creating the planning group. Each person appointed should be there for a purpose and should be able to make a substantial contribution. There are three critical elements in assembling a group—the size of the group, the nature of the group, and the selection of a leader. Let's review each one.

Size of the group: A planning group can be anywhere from two to eight people. Two people would be proper for change that is minor or confidential. The larger the group, the less chance of maintaining confidentiality. Change that will have a substantial impact could require eight people. Obviously, a larger group has more people to share the workload. If the change is substantial and/or difficult, more people make it more likely that all aspects of the change will be considered.

Planning begins to deteriorate with more than eight in the group. Serious communication and problem-solving cannot occur. Large groups tend to form sub-groups, making it difficult to band people together as one group only. If the project does require more than eight people, consider the eight people as master planners. Each of the master planners could chair a sub-committee of people not in the main planning group. These sub-committees can receive specific charges from the master planners while still allowing the master planners to remain as one group. Larger groups are for information sharing only.

The nature of the group: Next, look at who will serve on the group. One of the most common questions people ask is how to get staff to accept change. The answer lies here. If those most affected by the change are appointed to the planning group, they will be likely to accept the change more readily. After all, the planning group now "owns" the change. Unless the change must be kept confidential from the staff, appoint the people affected to the planning group.

A good planning group also contains a mix of talents. Obviously, if the change is technical, then technical people should be involved. But strive for a blend of people so that there are people who are creative, people who have a broad perspective, and people who understand the day-to-day reality. Each person approaches the problem from a different point of view, and each one rescues the others from becoming too mired in their specialty.

Selection of a leader: The selection of the leader, or chairperson, is pivotal. The library manager may not be the best person to chair the planning group, for several reasons. First, the change may not be of sufficient significance to occupy the manager's time. Second, it gives staff a chance to feel responsible and influential over the directions of the organization, which enhances their self-worth and self-esteem. Third, a manager's presence may inhibit honest discussion. For example, if the change involves cleaning up a problem, staff may protect their co-workers by covering up information. A manager must weigh what type of change is expected before deciding to be a part of the group.

If it has been decided to choose a chairperson who is not the manager, look for these characteristics: first and foremost is an ability to get things done. If the change is on a large scale, the person should have a proven record of achievement. Otherwise, management may want to gamble on an upcoming person who has the raw material for leadership. This person should be a positive thinker who is committed to the project, who has broad perspective, and who has credibility with the staff. Remember not to confuse popularity with credibility. Popularity refers to how well a person is liked; credibility refers to how believeable a person is.

STEP 2
Set parameters

Managing the task itself is only half the work. Management of the planning group also requires setting parameters for the group. Many times, managers will simply assemble the group and expect the task to be done. That may work with high-level administrators, but it will not be a successful technique in general. For most groups, it is better to clearly define the group's authority, confidentiality, and participation.

The authority of the group: A manager must decide and state up-front the scope of the group's authority. It must be clear whether the group has decision-making authority or is only advisory. Do not fall into the trap of creating a group, giving its members the impression that they have a lot of authority, and then discounting their work. It is a sure-fire way to build resentment and create early problems with change.

Confidentiality: Change that has to do with personnel issues, reorganizations, reclassifications, or union matters is by its very nature confidential. Unless the organization has clear policies, the manager must decide on what may or may not be shared. Generally speaking, the more open an organization, the more successful it is. But it is not possible to be open about all things. Be honest with the group about what they must keep confidential and about what is kept confidential from them. Never let a group assume they know all when, in fact, whole areas are not available to them. They will feel foolish and come to resent the manager. People understand confidentiality and appreciate honesty.

Participation: Managers should always be students of group behavior. They must be very knowledgeable about how groups work and must ensure a certain level of participation among members of the group. Without strong participation, the best work of a group cannot be done.

It is quite common for people to be in groups and not participate. People sometimes join committees for their performance evaluations or their résumés. Also, people vary considerably in their energy levels as well as in their ability to speak up and to take risks in a group. The leader must make sure that all are participating and sharing the work load equally.

There are many different styles for working with groups, and the manager may wish to explore several of them. Whatever technique is used, the goal should be to get people to consider ideas before judging them. Creative work can only occur in a safe environment. An idea should be considered for its merits and never condemned out of hand. The group will need to learn to build on ideas, not destroy them. When people feel safe to speak their mind, they will participate on a regular basis.

A manager must also be conscious of the roles that people play in groups. People do assume different behaviors at different times. Some of that behavior is constructive, some is destructive. Observe what type of roles people are acting out and whether or not their behavior contributes to the well-being and productivity of the group. Watch for excessive straying from the agenda, tearing down the ideas of others, or failing to take the project seriously. Do not hesitate to speak to people about counter-productive behavior. Such behavior must be stopped.

STEP 3
Build a team

Since the management of change is a group process, a manager needs to be concerned with welding the planning group into a team. The spirit that comes with teamwork will have a beneficial effect on even the most trying of changes.

Before discussing how to build teams, let's look at what teams are not. Teams are not large groups of people. Neither are they permanent. They come together for a common purpose and then disband. The illusion, popular with managers, that their staff is a team is a fallacy. Their staff may operate as a team from time to time, but not on a regular basis. Teams are built when there is a common goal, when there is a sense of importance and pride in the work, when there is vitality, support, a liking for the task, and a sense of accomplishment. Let's look at each one of these aspects.

The single unifying factor that makes a team a team is a common goal. People united to achieve a purpose are capable of developing a dynamic work group. A manager needs to give the group a clear goal that looks, however challenging, to be accomplishable. The manager creates the vision that will spur the team on.

Teams form when a group has a sense of importance and pride in the task. The value of the goal to the organization should be carefully spelled out. When staff gain prestige, which is an intrinsic reward, they become bonded together by the uniqueness and richness of the purpose. Of course, a good manager must be careful not to create an elitist group.

Vitality is another ingredient of a good team. A manager cannot give vitality, but can show it. The compelling nature of the goal can command it. This vitality will also make people feel close to each other. Intense, shared experiences are long remembered.

Teamwork also comes when people are supportive of each other. To be a team means to be together. People who are critical or cynical will impede the forging of a team. A team, by its very nature, is for the good of the whole. The team takes diverse talents and unifies them into a cohesive force. A team needs people who are constructive and who cheer each other on.

A team is also built on a liking for the task. It does little good to put global, creative thinkers into a job that needs painstaking attention to detail. They will never have the heart for it, no matter how much they may struggle to overcome their feelings. Build a team around people who are interested.

A group becomes bonded into a team when they begin to see some accomplishments. People need success for self-esteem. If they can see some progress, they will develop a feeling of effectiveness. This feeds on itself. A person with a string of accomplishments will continue to be successful.

Finally, managers should remember to be team players themselves. A positive outlook—vital, sure of purpose, and resilient in the face of problems—is characteristic of a team leader.

STEP 4
Plan the first meeting

The importance of first impressions is never so evident as during the first meeting. If it is well-organized, with clear directions and a sense of vitality, the committee members will feel that they are involved in a project of worth and value. They will make the necessary initial commitment to the project.

If, on the other hand, the meeting is disorganized, late, and unclear, the committee members will soon be discouraged or frustrated. If that image is carried back to the rest of the staff, which it will be, the change will soon become something to ridicule.

A skillful manager will plan the initial meeting meticulously to give the fledgling project every chance to survive. Let's look at the aspects that need consideration.

Setting agendas: One of the reasons that meetings fail so often is that they are disorganized. Meetings should have set agendas with time frames and should list the goal or the product of each section. Readings should be sent out prior to the meeting. The agenda, which should go out no less than three days before the meeting, should state what to bring that will help the meeting. Other notes can also be made on agendas, such as location information, if the staff is unfamiliar with that facility, or parking directions.

A good agenda helps people organize their thoughts prior to the meeting. It also creates an impression of the level of organization that will be expected and the serious purpose of the project.

Note that agendas for subsequent meetings should have minutes of the previous meeting attached and should list items that need action.

Physical lay-out of the first meeting: Do not arrive scant moments before the first meeting and accept whatever physical lay-out is available. The proximity and configuration of seating can have a dramatic effect upon people. One cannot evoke thoughtful interaction among people who are too far apart or seated in an irregular pattern. The manager should create a circle or square of tables and get people face to face. People need room, of course, for papers and movement, but all need to feel they are sitting within a group. Where people sit may also be of interest to the manager. People who sit closer to the chairperson are usually more in agreement. The farther away a person sits, the less agreement unless the person is directly opposite the chairperson. That person could be in opposition or completely in support. A manager must test such situations until they feel workable.

Working with the chairperson: Prior to the first meeting, the manager should sit down with the chairperson (assuming that the manager is not chairing the meeting) to make sure that the group leader fully understands the task and the expectations. This is a step all too often skipped. The manager should also set up regular meeting times with the chairperson so there is a steady flow of communication. The group leader should feel free to communicate with the manager at all times.

The task of the first meeting: The manager should attend at least part of the first meeting and talk about what is to be achieved. Discussions should be free-form and extensive. This is where people begin to clarify what is wanted. Devote as much time to this as possible.

At this first meeting, timeframes should be established. Make sure they are realistic. Be prepared to negotiate times unless there are major external reasons not to alter them. Also discuss the resources needed and be supportive of requests. High-level managers should be able to provide most of their own resources but make sure that they realize the extent of authorization. Time can also be a resource. Managers must take care that they have not overloaded their star performers.

A manager should also clarify the sequence of action. This will enable staff to see the project through to the end. Checkpoints can be created at this time so that the manager can follow the group's progress.

Remember also to give staff the contextual framework of the change. Review with the planning group the thinking that went on in Conceptualizing. It will be the responsibility of the planning group to take that vision, modify or adapt it, and use it to formulate the goals of the change.

At this point the manager should not hesitate to talk about change in general. One of the most difficult aspects of change is that we are frequently called upon to re-invent the wheel. During the process of change, a great deal of discovery and self-discovery will occur. While such revelations can be good, they can also be painful. A great deal of this pain can be avoided when awareness occurs before the event takes place. Therefore, talk about change in depth so the planning group can anticipate events.

CONCLUSION

Organizing the task force is a necessary, although often overlooked, aspect of the change process. While these steps appear simple, they play an important part in assembling the right group of people to plan and implement the change. The price of a casual approach to organizing the planning group will not be immediately obvious, but will take on more importance as it becomes increasingly evident that the change is not progressing smoothly. Take the time to organize the best planning group possible in the best way possible. This also shows the staff the way that the manager expects them to proceed.

QUICK CHECK

STEP 1
Assemble the planning group

A. What size group is needed?
B. How will the group be chosen?
C. Who will be selected leader?

STEP 2
Set parameters

A. What will the authority of the group be?
B. How confidential is the project?
C. What behavior is expected?

STEP 3
Build a team

A. Does the team have a sense of the importance of the task?
B. Are the members supportive of each other?
C. Does the staff have a liking for the task?
D. Does the team have a sense of vitality?

STEP 4
Plan the first meeting

A. Has an agenda been set?
B. Has the chairperson met with the manager?
C. Has the physical arrangement of the room been considered?
D. Has the goal of the first meeting been established?

4 PLANNING

STEP 1
Develop the vision

STEP 2
Create options

STEP 3
Evaluate options

STEP 4
Choose an option

STEP 5
Write the goals and objectives

STEP 6
Develop the plan

Think of the management of change as a journey. To conceptualize is to decide where to go. To plan is to decide how to get there. It is the planning process that brings ideas into being. Good planning reveals the depth of commitment and organizational skills of a manager and is essential for smooth implementation. If a project is cohesive and well-organized, people will have a positive attitude about change. Projects poorly planned often fail and cause considerable frustration amongst the staff.

The manager's responsibility is to guide the planning group through the planning sequence. Since no step should be skipped, it is a good idea to have the planning group report after each step. It is a common failing of committees to rush ahead to implement parts of the change before the necessary groundwork has been done. There are six steps in the planning process.

STEP 1
Develop the vision

During conceptualization, the manager has thought deeply about the change and has created a preliminary vision. It will be the task of the planning group to re-trace the manager's thinking and adapt, modify, or re-create a vision within that framework. The difference is that the manager's vision set a direction in a general way. The planning group's vision will develop the details and finishing touches so everyone has a specific sense of what the change will be like.

It is important at this time for the planning group to delve deeply into whatever problem made the change surface. Of course, not all change occurs as a result of a problem, but most does. For example, frequent complaints by patrons about the collection or service is a signal that change is needed. A new housing development on the edge of town, ten miles from the closest public library, will initiate a change to develop service for that community. All change responds to a need. The planning group has to be absolutely clear on what the need is.

If the problem is not understood completely, the change will be skewed. Unfortunately, as every experienced manager knows, often the problem that is seen on the surface is not the real problem. Careful thought is required to get at the roots of a problem since all planning must stem from a correct interpretation of events. Problem identification is particularly treacherous when there are behaviorial problems or problems between staff members. There, conflicting opinions as to rights and wrongs will prove confusing and misleading. It is very difficult when a manager must rely on potentially prejudiced information. Obviously, people in a conflict situation will not be objective reporters. The planning group needs to investigate the problem thoroughly, hear all opinions, and gather all the facts. A manager who feels that the problem is very difficult should try to observe the situation first hand. There is simply no substitute for personal observation.

If the change is of any magnitude, the manager needs to consider having the planning group carry out future research. Future research, simply put, is an analysis of the probability that certain significant trends will affect a particular organization. Before the vision is in place, have the planning group scan the environment to determine what is occurring and what is pending in the marketplace that will affect the destiny of the service undergoing change. This is particularly important when plans are being developed for long-range technological change. For example, what will be the eventual impact on reference services when a global information utility is bounced worldwide off a satellite? What will happen to books when laser discs hit their full stride? Will "smart" buildings be able to guide patrons to the section they need?

Not all change, obviously, will deal with such big issues. Most change will deal with the near future, such as projections for a new housing development or mall, or perhaps a new version of software expected out next year. The important thing is for the planning group to look to the horizon and to attempt to ascertain what in the future will affect the change.

Two points must be made here. First of all, organizations can and do shape their own futures. It is important to have a positive attitude and think strategically. While broad social changes sweep all of us along, we are not dust in the wind. Organizations must play a dynamic role in their own destiny.

Second, remember, when looking at future trends, to talk only in terms of probabilities. No one can predict the future, despite what might appear on the best seller list. There are only probabilities, likelihoods, and the certainty of change.

Although it will be difficult, the planning group should commit the vision to writing with some explanation of their underlying thought process. That vision will be used again and again throughout planning, implementing, and evaluating. If it is not written down, the vision will be dependent upon human memory. In time, memory will fade and the vision will be lost.

STEP 2
Create Options

Once the vision has been defined, the next step will be to create as many options as possible to achieve the vision. Remember that there are always several paths to every target, and the planning group needs examine them all. For example, let's say that the circulation of an inner-city library is declining and the manager and the planning group have decided that they do not want to accept the downward trend. Their vision is a viable, well-used, and dynamic library. What are the options here? More programs? A better collection? More staff? Stronger outreach?

It might be that all paths are viable ways to achieve the vision. The important thing is to assemble as many options as possible.

Managers may ask themselves how to get a planning group to generate such a wealth of ideas. Of the many techniques for idea-generation in groups, there are three that a manager can rely upon to consistently produce results: brainstorming, sub-grouping, and the nominal group technique. These are most effective for a planning group already assembled and working together. Let's look at each one:

Brainstorming: Brainstorming is such a commonly used word that it frequently surprises people to hear that it is a formal group technique with its very own rules. So effective is brainstorming that a manager should learn to use it well. The process is quite straight-forward.

Once the group is assembled, the manager must explain clearly why ideas must be generated. This explanation must also include any background or pertinent facts as well as a brief analysis of the significance of this issue to the organization. Now, obviously, if the group is the same group that has been involved in developing the vision, such detail will not be necessary. Nevertheless, a manager should not be afraid of repetition as it will give clarity each time the planning group embarks upon another step.

Once the purpose has been clearly stated, the manager should proceed to explain that brainstorming is a technique for idea-generation, but that it works only when the group adheres to the rules. To be effective, the following rules should be observed:

> Any idea on the topic is welcome even if it sounds frivolous or unworkable.
> Any idea can be built upon by another member of the group, but no idea may be discarded yet by the group.
> No idea can be judged at the time it is presented. Premature judging of ideas will stifle the flow of additional ideas, particularly for the person who presented the idea.

All of the ideas that are suggested must be recorded automatical-ly on a flipchart. The recorder does not select what does or does not go onto the flipchart. Any hesitation to record an idea is the same as premature judging and will have the same result.

One key to successful brainstorming is for the manager to create an atmosphere of enthusiasm and fun. People generally love the creative process. A group leader must trigger that natural impulse and encourage people to call out their ideas no matter how outlandish. The goal for now is to gather as many ideas as possible.

Another key to effective brainstorming is to explain to the group the importance of separating themselves from the idea. Frequently, a person whose idea is rejected suffers a little erosion of self-esteem. A manager needs to move the group towards creative maturity so people can put their ideas before the group without negative consequences. It is up to the manager to see that people who generate ideas do not get beaten up in meetings. When the whole group follows the rules of brainstorming carefully, ideas will flow with no damage to the participants.

The manager will also note an ebb and flow to the creative process. There will be a lot of ideas at first and then a lull. Do not be afraid of quiet times, as they usually mean that people are getting ready to build upon the ideas of others or are making links between ideas. Use intuition to tell when the group is getting ready for a second round or when they are done. Be sure to allow plenty of time for the brainstorming process. Not only is this step vital, but it also is among the more pleasurable aspects of managing change. The pleasure and intensity of the experience will bond the group and help them work effectively afterwards.

At the conclusion of brainstorming, when the group is done and all ideas are recorded, then everyone can begin evaluating the suggestions. How that evaluation occurs will be discussed in detail in Step 3.

Sub-grouping: Sub-grouping is another effective way to generate ideas and is often used in conjunction with brainstorming. Normally, sub-grouping is used with groups that are too large or groups that are shy. If the manager has had to appoint a group that is larger than the recommended maximum of eight, or finds that people are not comfortable speaking out before others, then sub-grouping should be considered.

As with brainstorming, the manager begins by stating clearly the issue to be addressed and by explaining the background and the pertinent facts. After that, the manager can go one of two ways: either the sub-groups will have the same issue to consider or each sub-group will have a part of the issue. For example, if we address again the problem of declining usage at an inner-city library, the manager could ask each sub-group to address the total problem or to address an aspect of it such as lack of attendance at storytimes, poor magazine circulation, or low turnover of bestsellers. Breaking a problem or a vision into small parts is particularly effective with large projects. Of course, this means that, before the meeting, the manager must prepare assignments for each sub-group and must explain each assignment clearly.

Forming sub-groups can be tricky. Since it is an over-used technique, many people have a lot of resistance to it. If the manager is sure, however, that it is the best technique, it is important to divide the group carefully. The most effective way is letting people volunteer for the areas of discussion that attract them. Although this frequently creates an imbalance in the sub-grouping—i.e., five people in one and two on another—it has the advantage of utilizing people's motivation. Another effective way is to count off. Whatever number a person gets determines their sub-group. Staff usually respond to the fairness and structure of this technique. Do not permit sub-grouping to become chaotic. If it does, then the manager needs to assess whether the staff is resisting the process or the assignment. Open up communication at that point for feedback from the planning group.

Once sub-groups are formed and assignments given, the sub-groups can begin brainstorming their specific issue. The rules of brainstorming need to be explained and a person selected to act as recorder of ideas generated. The manager also needs to set a realistic time limit for the group's work.

Once the sub-group has finished, the recorder presents their ideas to the other sub-groups. This is the spot where sub-grouping frequently breaks down. The tedium of listening to people relay lists of ideas can sap the group's vitality. The manager must make sure the recorders move through their lists rapidly but effectively. Allowing everyone to add other ideas or request a clarification while the recorder is speaking will help alleviate boredom. The various lists must then be integrated and common threads identified. Then the evaluation of ideas can begin.

The major disadvantage of sub-grouping is that it alters the nature of the primary group. Groups form rapidly, so the manager must take care that the members of the planning group identify with the group as a whole rather than with the sub-group. Sub-grouping can be disruptive to the flow of a meeting because the group must first come together as a main group, re-form as sub-groups, and then form once again as a main group. As with any enterprise, focus is the key to success, and sub-grouping does create a break in the concentration.

However, its benefits often outweigh its disadvantages. The most obvious benefit is that a small, motivated group can be very productive and creative. In addition, people who may not speak up in a group, even as small as a group of eight, will speak up with two or three other people. So in sub-grouping everyone will make a contribution. Lastly, because the groups are small, people will tend to speak more honestly, and honest communication is a firm bedrock for the management of change. Managers can also use people in the sub-groups to form standing sub-committees if the change is large enough to warrant a division of assignments.

Nominal Group Technique: Like sub-grouping, the nominal group technique can be used for larger groups or for groups that tend to be quiet. However, it can also be used effectively in small groups. It is a process designed to allow everyone in the group to put forward their ideas and be heard equally.

Once again, the manager begins by explaining the issue, the background, and the pertinent facts. Then the planning group is asked to take a few minutes to write down all their ideas on this subject. In other words, the individual brainstorms alone generating as many ideas as possible. Quiet must be observed in the room during this process.

When everyone in the group has stopped writing, the group leader asks each person in turn to tell their first idea and records all the ideas on a flip chart. After each person has given one idea, the manager goes around again for second ideas, third, fourth, and so on until all the ideas are recorded. People may pass on any of the rounds if they have offered all of their ideas or if their ideas have already been mentioned by someone else. Once again, at this point no judging of ideas is permitted. However, once all the ideas are up, people should proceed to build upon the ideas of others.

The advantage of the nominal group technique is that it allows everyone an equal opportunity to have their ideas heard. It is a particularly good technique in groups that have two or three people who are more verbally agile than others. It permits the quiet ones to speak and forces the more talkative ones to listen.

The only real disadvantage of this technique is that it does not generate the warmth and spontaneity that brainstorming does. Initially, because of its formal structure, it can seem to be a rather stately process. The group leader may want to consider having two recorders so that the flow of ideas onto the flip charts is continual. Brainstorming can be used after all the ideas are recorded. Note that with all of these techniques the essential ingredient is respect for what the other person has to say.

A manager should use brainstorming, sub-grouping, and the nominal group technique with confidence because of their consistent reliability and effectiveness. Understand, however, that working with groups is a learning process both for the group and for the manager. If the manager does not have much experience in working with groups, there will be a learning period before that manager can really make a group hum. The key to working with groups is to think through what the meeting should accomplish and then think through a strategy, preferably a flexible one, that will meet these goals. True learning in a group comes about when all the members learn to hear and see themselves in relationship to others. Active listening and awareness are vital.

A word of caution for any manager about to embark upon a group technique: There are dozens of different techniques available, but most are overly stylized. An unnecessarily cumbersome technique can easily subvert the mission of the group. When the technique is too complicated, the planning group will either become too involved in learning the process or too lost in the rigid and complex structure of the technique. Both consequences will deter idea generation. All of us have had the experience of being in a group led by a leader with a newly minted facilitator certificate, and being forced to stay with a process that was clearly unworkable. If the group is not responsive to a particular technique, the manager should discard it immediately.

STEP 3
Evaluate the options

In order to choose the best path, options must be rigorously evaluated. It would be a waste of time to proceed with choices that are unrealistic. Test each option against these questions:

> Does the option have a systems perspective?
> Does the option support the goals of the organization?
> Was the environment considered?
> Are all the resources available to this option?
> Does the option coincide with the stated mission of the library?
> Have personal goals influenced this option?

DOES THE OPTION HAVE A SYSTEMS PERSPECTIVE?

Every part of an organization is related to another. To affect one part is to affect another. Oftentimes, change is planned in a vacuum. An idea might be very good for one unit, but not for another.

Be sure that the planning group recognizes the interrelationships within the organization. If a goal developed here bumps another important goal or damages another unit or division, then it must be rejected unless it is so worthwhile that the secondary unit must change also.

IS THE OPTION SUPPORTIVE OF THE GOALS OF THE ORGANIZATION?

Since the option will eventually form the goal, consider whether it will support the other goals of the organization.

Goals should form a network that is mutually supportive. Consider not only the goals of the project, but also the goals of the organization. Every goal should be towards a central purpose and not in conflict with any other goal. If a conflict occurs, one part of the organization may end up working against another, which will cause both a waste of resources and confusion amongst the staff.

WAS THE ENVIRONMENT CONSIDERED?

Every library has an internal environment and exists in an external environment. Environment refers to the political, social, economic, and technological events within or outside of the library. One must consider the receptivity of the surroundings to a goal. Sometimes, no matter how desirable a change is, the environment will not accept it. For example, the manager may need to create additional parking spaces for patrons who have been complaining about lacking a place to park. But if the Board of Trustees is very worried about budget, they may not approve that expenditure. A transfer for several staff members might be a good idea, but if contract negotiations are occurring, staff may be suspicious of management motives. This does not mean that a manager should be intimidated or controlled by the environment, but skill in gauging timing or in preparing it to receive changes is needed.

ARE ALL THE RESOURCES AVAILABLE TO THIS OPTION?

Although a change in the organization may require various resources, two are of paramount importance—budget and personnel. Major change costs both time and money. It is not uncommon for a library to have adequate staff for current services but not enough to support a new project. A library that is part of a governmental entity also frequently finds itself in a hiring freeze, or unable to obtain needed personnel even when budget is available.

If all the resources are not available, that does not mean the project has to stop. Obtaining resources can be part of the implementation strategy. However, do not proceed without adequate resources, as the project will be damaged by undercapitalization. A message will also be sent to the staff that the project is not important enough to be staffed adequately or to have adequate resources.

IS THERE A STRUCTURE TO SUPPORT THE OPTION?

Public, academic, and school libraries, in particular, have many codes and contracts that control expenditures, classification levels of personnel, and revenues. If a proposed change is entrepreneurial, it is very possible that the organization will not have the structure in place to support the idea. For example, what if a library seeks to charge fees for some services or decides to sell a product? There are codes controlling commercialization of services. Consider how the idea relates to the existing nature of the organization, and how that structure might be changed to accommodate the idea.

DOES THE OPTION COINCIDE WITH THE STATED MISSION OF THE LIBRARY?

Every library has a central purpose. Although the fundamentals of librarianship remain the same, the particulars can vary widely. Some libraries are popular, some specialized, some archival, and some research-related. There would have to be exceptional circumstances to justify a small public library developing a rare book collection or an archive opening a popular reading room. Neither of these events would relate to the library's central mission.

HAVE PERSONAL GOALS INFLUENCED THIS OPTION?

Many times people launch projects to further themselves without reference to the overall good of the organization. While ambitious individuals are good for organizations, they can sometimes set or influence goals more for personal than organizational benefit. A high-level manager can skew an organization easily if personal goals consistently intrude.

STEP 4
Choose an option

After evaluating all the options, there are usually one or two that are the best choices, that best suit the needs and requirements of the vision. Depending upon the authority of the planning group, they can either choose an option or recommend one to the manager. A recommendation should list the pros and cons of each option, with a rationale for the top choice. No alternative can be 100% positive; the negatives must also be considered. In giving preliminary approval, the manager must consider whether the benefits outweigh the costs. Costs, of course, are not just financial expenditures. They can include such things as staff morale, too much turmoil at work, or the utilization of too many resources.

Please note that this is still only a preliminary approval stage. The manager's review prevents the staff from investing too much time and other resources in a project that the manager may think is no longer feasible. The final decision will come later, when the planning is completed.

STEP 5
Write the goals and objectives

The planning group will need to develop goals based upon the options, preferably goals that are quantifiable or at least easily evaluated and measured. Clearly stated goals are critical to the success of change. Most of a manager's life is involved with goal-setting. It seems easy, but clearly remains a problem. Do not let the planning group get lost in discussions of what are goals and what are objectives. Simply put, goals are statements of what is wanted. For example, if there are complaints about poor service at the reference desk, the vision would include descriptions of friendly and efficient service. Various options, such as accuracy of questions, more staff, and better collection, would have been itemized. The goals would be more specific and would refer to such things as a 90% accuracy rate in answers or 95% customer satisfaction. The objectives would lead to the goals and would include areas such as training in customer relations, telephone etiquette, or data-base searching.

Initially, the planning group should spend a large part of its time on goal setting. It will be important through the life of the project and afterward to be able to state with the utmost clarity what the goals were.

Writing goals is not easy, but not impossible either. Goals state:

> who. . .
> does what. . .
> with what result. . .
> by when. . .

Goals should evoke in a reader's mind a clear picture of what will occur. Remember that goals should always state results, not process. For example, if the manager wanted to increase the pages' shelving speed, the goal should state that the pages will shelve 70 books per hour. A process goal states that there will be a workshop to train the pages to shelve faster. Notice that the first one has tangible results, but the second does not.

Goals should also form a hierarchy. If the project is relatively complex, there should be major goals and then sub-goals. This will help in the implementation.

There are two major pitfalls to watch out for. The first of these is language. Since people imbue words with their own experiences, each word has a different shade of meaning to different people. It is best to try out the goal statement on several people to see if everyone has the same understanding.

The second problem is a chronic tendency to shift goals halfway through a project, to bring one goal into ascendancy, or to choose a goal towards the end. Projects will take on a life of their own, and many pressures will be brought to bear upon people to modify goals. When such goal displacement occurs, the integrity of the project will be eroded and credibility of management damaged. Goal displacement refers to goals that are at cross-purposes with the overall mission of the organization. If a manager sees that a shift is necessary, it is best to be open about making a change and to state it publicly. Remember that the goals should drive the project, not vice versa.

Note that this process is top-down management. There is much to be said for goals being created at all levels on the organization. Although many libraries have a decided preference for goals coming only from below, the broad goals and directions need to come from management.

STEP 6
Develop the plan

Once the goals have been agreed upon and written down, the planning group must proceed to develop the plan for the change. Eventually, this plan will be turned into a written report for the manager to review. The plan, and the report, must contain the following elements:

    A. Background
    B. Vision, Goals and Objectives
    C. Design
    D. Implementation Plan
    E. Budget
    F. Schedule

A. BACKGROUND

In this section, the planning group should review how the project came about and why. There should also be an explanation of the assumptions that were made about the change so all readers can understand the basis upon which decisions were made.

B. VISION, GOALS AND OBJECTIVES

Since the vision, the goals, and the objectives show the direction of the change, they should be stated at the beginning to provide the framework for the entire plan.

C. DESIGN

The design will take most of the planning group energy. The design will show what the change will look like in as detailed a fashion as possible. For example, say that a public library chooses as a goal the establishment of bookmobile service to a rural area, then the planning group must consider such questions as:

> the type of van to obtain
> the amount and level of staff
> the frequency of service
> the nature of the collection
> the publicity campaign
> the route

In addition, the design should contain many internal organizational issues such as:

> the location of desks for new staff
> the ordering of supplies for the bookmobile
> the reporting structure for the staff
> the telephone installations
> the location of book drops

In other words, when designing change, design it completely. Do not defer problems or leave out details. Every issue raised must be resolved here. Leave as little as possible to chance.

D. THE IMPLEMENTATION PLAN

The implementation plan contains the instructions for the staff about how the change, as it is designed, will be implemented. This step is often left until the implementation phase, but by that time it is too late because problems in the implementation plan can halt the change. When the group is developing the plan, it is a wiser investment of staff time to plan it completely. Let's take an example that shows the difference between design and implementation. Say that an academic library has a space problem, and a decision has been made to rearrange one of the floors of the library. In design, we would have thought ahead to what this would require, asking ourselves such questions as:

How much shelving?
What is the lay-out?
What will be the impact upon the patrons?
Will the floor plan have to be re-published?
How will the work flow be affected?
Will the pattern of lighting be sufficient?
Will the staff have adequate visual control?
Will the shelving be clockwise or counterclockwise?

In the implementation plan would be such issues as:

Who will order additional shelving?
Which stacks should be moved first?
How will patrons be re-routed?
Who will update the directory?
Who will direct the move?

The design and the implementation are two sides of the same coin. The planning group should develop a comprehensive plan for both.

E. BUDGET

Here, the planning group will consider the real costs to the organization. The budget should include materials, equipment, and staff. In addition, make sure that there is a contingency fund for emergencies. The larger and more complex the change, the larger the contingency fund should be.

F. THE TIMETABLE

This is the schedule for approval and implementation. The greatest potential problem here is not allowing enough time. The timetable must be driven by the demands of the work. Do not permit the timetable to drive the task unless there is an exceptionally good reason for the goals to be accomplished within a certain timeframe. An accelerated timetable will cause the staff stress and erode the quality of the project.

All of these elements should be included in a written report and submitted to the manager. The planning group should also add any other considerations, such as possible negative or political consequences. The manager needs as full a picture as possible to ensure that there will be no surprises that will deter the change.

CONCLUSION

Careful and controlled planning ensures successful change. It is imperative to consider every detail and to be as thorough as necessary. Quality planning brings out all the necessary dimensions of the change and forestalls many future difficulties. The greatest failing of all planning groups is lack of steadiness. People grow weary of the detail needed for planning and rush ahead to implementation. Planning that has not been well thought out will create more problems and will cost the organization more in the long run. The manager must ensure that quality work is done on this phase.

QUICK CHECK

STEP 1
Develop the vision

A. Has the problem been correctly identified?
B. Has the vision been committed to writing?

STEP 2
Create options

A. Have all the options been considered?
B. Did the manager allow the planning group to generate as many ideas as possible?

STEP 3
Evaluate the options

A. Does the option have a system perspective?
B. Is the option supportive of the goals of the organization?
C. Was the environment considered?
D. Are all the resources available to this option?
E. Is there a structure to support the option?
F. Does the option coincide with the stated mission of the library?
G. Have personal goals influenced this option?

STEP 4
Choose an option

A. Does the group have the authority to make a choice?
B. If the manager makes the choice, is there enough information for a good decision?

STEP 5
Write the goals and objectives

A. Are the goals quantifiable?
B. Do the goals state who does what, by when and with what result?
C. Are the goals clear to everyone?
D. Are the goals in line with the vision?

STEP 6
Develop the plan

A. Has the plan been written down for the manager?
B. Has the design included every aspect?
C. Has an implementation plan been included?
D. Is the timetable realistic?

5 DECIDING

STEP 1
Review all documents

STEP 2
Evaluate the pros and cons

STEP 3
Consider the consequences

STEP 4
Allow for mature deliberation

STEP 5
Avoid barriers

STEP 6
Make the right decision

After the change has been planned and the design is satisfactory to the planning group, the manager must review what has been done up to this point and decide whether or not to proceed.

It is important for a manager to take time to review the change in-depth. It is also important that the period of decision-making occur after planning but before the implementing. If implementing is underway, there will be too much waste of staff time. If the decision falls before planning, there might not be enough facts to see how feasible the change will be.

Let's look for a moment at what decision-making actually is. A decision is a means to an end because it moves the organization forward to a desired goal. An organization prospers on a series of good decisions. Moreover, so do library managers. An effective manager makes effective decisions.

Generally speaking, there are two types of decisions. The first is routine. These decisions are made on a regular basis and have many rules and regulations to cover them. The second is the non-routine. This is the arena in which a library manager usually dwells. Many of these decisions are fraught with ambiguity: that is, the situations could have a number of interpretations. Ambiguous situations by definition do not present a clear choice. The higher a person goes, the more complex and ambiguous decision-making becomes. Most major change, naturally enough, falls into the non-routine category. One reason ambiguous situations are so difficult is that we permit the complexity to overwhelm us and to cloud our decision-making. However, decision-making has a logical sequence which, if followed, will greatly increase the manager's chances of making the best decision. Let's look now at the five steps involved in making a decision on change.

STEP 1
Review all documents

The manager should have the full recommendation of the planning group before proceeding to review the documents. The manager should study all documents that relate to the change. In the course of a project with which the manager is familiar, it is very tempting to skim such a report. However, a careful manager should set aside time to thoroughly read and review the report. Problem areas should be noted and questioned. This is the time to follow-through and correct any potentially difficult situations.

If the managers were not in the planning group, they may want to consider having the planning group make a presentation of the report. There are nuances to an oral report that do not occur in a written report. Additionally, any problems can be cleared up at the time of the meeting. Of course, the manager should have read the report in advance of the presentation and should not feel compelled to make a decision on the spot. Staff generally have positive feelings about giving reports orally as it is recognition for their good work. Be sure to praise the report first and then question afterwards.

Even if there will be no presentation, the manager should have some discussion with the key staff on the planning group. Ask them how they feel now about the project, what their main concerns are, and if they feel certain about the recommendations that they have made. People will transmit information in person that they will not commit to writing. This is particularly true of negative information. Negative information can be softened by speech, whereas the same information in writing can seem very harsh. People often eliminate negative information in written reports for that reason.

STEP 2
Evaluate the pros and cons

The final report from the planning group should spell out the pros and cons of the change. Even though the planning group should have closely evaluated these factors, the managers must now do the same. This is not to say that the work of the planning group is not good. It is simply to recognize the greater range of experience and broader perspective of most managers. In addition, most library managers are heavily involved in the political environment of their organization. They may be the only ones who have the complete picture of the acceptability of the change to boards of trustees, city councils, or corporate or academic vice-presidents. Weigh carefully the advantages and disadvantages of the change. Add others as they occur to create a balanced view. Make sure that the change is heavily weighted in advantages to the organization; otherwise it will not be worthwhile to move ahead.

STEP 3
Consider the consequences

It is one thing to make decisions, but another to live with the consequences. You must think through the consequences of any decision. How will the staff react? How will the faculty or students or patrons respond? A decision cannot be separated from its consequences.

For example, most library managers would agree that adding new staff is greatly to the advantage of a library. However, along with the positive results of greater service to patrons will also come the negative: upset from units that did not receive new staff, or controversy about the level of staff. Such consequences should not deter the managers from making a decision, but they must be foreseen and prepared for. Thinking change through completely helps to reduce strain on the organization.

STEP 4
Allow for mature deliberation

Mature deliberation can be defined as a period of time in which the project is allowed to rest so that thinking can ripen. Change frequently has an impulse all its own. People get caught up in it and begin to believe what has been set out regardless of contrary evidence. The library may have an excellent plan for change, but no plan is perfect. This period of mature deliberation allows the manager to reflect upon the project and make the decision to proceed. If, after this period, the change still looks good, then the change is desirable. If not, perhaps it was not as valuable as supposed.

Timing is everything in this phase. Too soon will be too quick for deliberation. Too long, and the project will slip away. Only the manager can sense the timing.

Deliberation should not be confused with a fear of decision-making. Managers are naturally cautious when making a decision that would have a substantial impact on the organization. The final responsibility lies with the manager, so some normal caution is to be expected. Only the manager may know when fear has replaced caution.

If a manager is normally a decisive person but has trouble making a particular decision, it might be wise to look for the reasons. Managers should respect their own executive intuition.

STEP 5
Avoid barriers

Every manager makes a bad decision at some point. Since effective management depends upon good decision-making, a bad decision shakes managers' confidence and causes them to ask why bad decisions occur. The answer is that there are many hidden barriers to decision-making. Managers must be skillful in recognizing and avoiding these barriers. Let's look at the major barriers to decision-making.

Insufficient facts: One main roadblock to good decision-making is having insufficient facts. It is usually impossible to have all the facts about any given situation, but it is important to have the critical data. Moreover, those facts must be accurate, or the conclusions will not be valid. Make sure that all the pertinent facts are marshaled.

Projected attitudes and values: The planning group must realize that individuals differ. While it is easy for a planning group to assume that everyone will act and feel as they do, the individuals about whom assumptions have been made may reject the change because they feel misunderstood.

The power of precedent: Precedent is a powerful force in organizations, particularly large ones such as corporate or government entities. A successful manager must calculate the influence of precedent on decision-making. A manager should not be afraid to break new ground, but must realize that precedent is a controlling force in both the manager's mind and in the minds of the staff.

The limitations of the rational process: Managers are only human. No matter how careful the planning, there are still limits to what is known and can be known. Sometimes decisions will not be good because there are limitations on the rational process. Good decision-making is based on the experiences of the past, not on a knowledge of the future. Not everything can be anticipated.

Opportunism: Beware of being unduly influenced by what may appear to be an opportunity. Libraries should be opportunistic only if it suits their overall mission and goals. A situation that looks good at first may not be right if it throws the organization out of kilter. Of course, libraries should be flexible, but they should not permit opportunism to upset the direction of the organization.

Pressure: Decision-making can sometimes be affected by undue pressure from boards, other executives, or staff. While such pressures merit serious weight, the manager must consider why the pressure is occurring. If it is simply pressure to speed up the decision-making, perhaps the organization is ready for change and the manager has delayed too long. However, if the pressure is for any gain other than the good of the organization, it should be withstood as skillfully as possible. This may be a little more difficult when the manager's supervisors are bringing the pressure.

Desire for perfection: Sometimes managers will delay decisions because they are perfectionists. Some projects require perfection; many do not. A manager may choose to accept the satisfactory or the very good rather than expending resources for an optimum plan in a situation that does not warrant that effort. This does not mean that a manager should not have high standards, but a balance must be struck between optimum results and optimum effort and satisfactory results and satisfactory effort.

The manager should acknowledge that these barriers exist and work through them. Understanding the limits of the decision-making process enables the manager to have realistic expectations.

STEP 6
Make the right decision

At this point, the manager has two choices—either proceed with the change or abort the process.

Hopefully, after all the thinking and planning that has occurred, the manager will decide to proceed with the change. This decision should be conveyed to the planning group, which will be eager to implement it. If the manager wants to proceed but needs modifications, that should also be communicated to staff at this time.

Sometimes, however, it is necessary for a manager to decide to abort the change. Aborted change is one aspect of the management of change. Although it is rarely discussed because people attach shame to failure, it can be a legitimate option for a manager. Aborting change is one of the toughest decisions a manager has to make. Let's look now at when and how change should be aborted.

WHEN SHOULD CHANGE BE ABORTED?
Change should be aborted when it is no longer feasible for the organization. Perhaps a sudden setback means redeploying staff and resources to another activity. If resources have been withdrawn, the change is no longer feasible and the manager should make a conscious decision to stop.

Change should also be aborted when it is no longer beneficial to the organization. Remembering the rule of thumb that all change should be beneficial, the manager should halt the change without hesitation if the benefit evaporates.

Generally, in aborted change, the manager makes a conscious decision to stop the change. However, change may also be aborted during turnovers of managers. Managers moving up in the organization may want to place their own stamp on the job and not complete work inherited from another. Managers coming in from outside may have a different perception of what the organization needs. Employees who have worked under a variety of managers and have had many projects disappear develop cynicism and an understandable reluctance to engage in any more such projects.

Sometimes, an incoming manager is not aware soon enough of a change underway. Change tends to come to a halt during a management turnover, and it may be difficult to pick up the threads again. This is more an accidental than a conscious decision to abort change, although the result is the same. New managers need to inquire about what projects are underway during the first week on the new job.

HOW TO ABORT CHANGE

Ideally, the planning group will agree with the manager that it is necessary to end the change.

If the change had importance to the organization, some explanation, but not apology, should be given to the staff. Good staff appreciate sound reasoning and will respond to the straightforwardness of management. Always disband change formally. This reduces the possibility of change appearing to disintegrate.

If the planning group or the staff at large does not agree with the manager, disbanding the change will be difficult. Although such circumstances do not occur very often, there are times when a manager will see things that the staff does not. An explanation should resolve disagreements. If not, the staff should be allowed to express their feelings of resentment and disappointment freely, but not indefinitely. When all is said and done, the manager has the right to decide. Of course, this is not a license to walk over the feelings of the staff, but everyone must go on to the next thing. Make every effort for staff to understand, however, as the manager's credibility might be called into question. Managers with questionable credibility can become objects of derision.

If the change was beneficial but no longer feasible, many managers are tempted to at least take the change through planning, reasoning that they will have the design should it ever be needed. It is better, however, to stop the change at whatever point it is no longer feasible. Staff turnovers, new technology, different environmental forces can alter thinking within a relatively short space of time. The work will be wasted, so it is better not to invest any further in it.

CONCLUSION

Once again, remember that an effective manager makes effective decisions. Good management rests on a firm foundation of skills of which decision-making is a cornerstone. Good decision-making calls for steadiness, common sense, experience, and sound intuition. It takes time to make good decisions. Decisions whose consequences have not been considered will often be regretted. Allow the right decisions to mature in their own time.

No manager should be afraid of aborting change, either. Although it is difficult to spend time on a project that does not bear fruit, it is still better than plunging the organization into nonbeneficial change. The test of good managers is their ability to handle the tough decisions.

QUICK CHECK

STEP 1
Review all documents

A. Did the manager read the reports completely?
B. Was a presentation made by staff?
C. Was the report discussed with staff?

STEP 2
Evaluate the pros and cons

A. Did the manager consider the advantages?
B. Did the manager consider the disadvantages?

STEP 3
Consider the consequences

A. Did the manager think about positive consequences?
B. Did the manager think about negative consequences?

STEP 4
Allow for mature deliberation

A. Did the manager allow the project to rest for awhile?
B. Is the timing good for the decision?
C. Did the manager allow a fear of decision-making to get in the way?

STEP 5
Avoid barriers

A. Were there insufficient facts?
B. Were there projected attitudes and values?
C. Was the power of precedent too influential?
D. Were the limitations of the rational process considered?
E. Was opportunism too influential?
F. Was there too much pressure?
G. Was there too much desire for perfection?

STEP 6
Make the right decision

A. Should the change proceed?
B. Should the change be aborted?

6 MANAGING THE INDIVIDUAL

STEP 1
Prepare for the meeting

STEP 2
Discuss the change

STEP 3
Keep the channels of communication open

STEP 4
Monitor performance

Organizations are more about people—their work habits, attitudes, and relationships—than about any thing else. An effective manager perceives an organization not as an entity, but as a network of people whose abilities, talents, and feelings combine to bring about library service. A manager looking at the structure of the organization should not see square blocks of units and departments, but instead people's names and faces—the same people who will be affected by change.

Change is difficult, change is easy. It depends upon individual reactions and the nature of the change. However, the successful integration of change into a library rests upon the manager's ability to manage people in change. In fact, the reason most change fails is that managers do not take people into account.

In order to effectively manage people, a manager must understand the sequence of feelings that a person experiences when confronted with change. These feelings will control much of the person's subsequent actions. When these feelings are known, they will explain a great deal of the individual's behavior. Instead of seeing anger, resentment, or depression as an abnormality on the part of the employee, the manager will know that this is part of the normal sequence of an individual accepting change. Of course, not all change is negative. Positive change also awakens feelings that must be treated with respect and care.

Sometimes people do not want to change, no matter how beneficial it might be. All managers have encountered the capable person who will not go for that promotion or will not take on additional responsibility. Managers deal almost daily with staff who will not learn a new procedure or who refuse to adapt to a new system. It is important for a manager to know how to manage people whose feelings against change overwhelm them and prohibit them from participating in the change process. In other words, managers have to know how to help people work through their feelings.

Often, hostility to change occurs at the moment the employee is informed about change. Many managers, because of nervousness or ignorance, handle this badly and aggravate an already difficult situation.

In this chapter, we will be discussing the proper way of informing the individual about change in order to gain the person's support and minimize resistance. Let's look at the steps a manager should take.

STEP 1
Prepare for the meeting

No manager should inform an employee about change without preparation. Change, negative change particularly, can have a dramatic effect upon an individual and upon that individual's relationship with the manager. When preparing, consider the time and place of the discussion, how to prepare the discussion, and how to anticipate reactions:

Time and place: The manager should choose a time that takes into account the schedule of the manager and the employee. No manager should conduct such a meeting in a hurry. The quality of the discussion will be eroded in the press of time.

The manager should also consider the subsequent events of the day. If the meeting could be emotional and confrontational, don't schedule it right before the employee goes on the reference desk or the manager goes to a press interview. Emotions need time to subside.

The manager should also consider the employee's personal life if the change is negative. If the person has just received word of a death in the family, that is not the time to inform him or her of an upsetting transfer. This is an issue of common courtesy between people.

Needless to say, all such conversations should be in confidential, private offices. If the manager has a modular or glass office where the employee response can be seen and heard, move the discussion to a meeting room, or even outside if necessary. This will spare the employee any embarrassment. Sending employees memos or stopping them in hallways are unacceptable practices.

Preparing the discussion: No manager should go into a meeting cold. Instead, think in advance about what needs to be said. Make sure you possess all the facts and know precisely how the employee will be affected and why. Consider also what summary you will give to conclude the meeting. Such mental preparation will allow you to do the best job and to remain in control of the situation if problems are expected.

Anticipating reactions: For all the talk about building humanistic organizations, an organization can still be a very callous place to work. Many times, we all get caught up in the tasks and goals and forget the human dimension. Never is this problem more evident than during change. Here the fast pace or the total involvement in the new and different causes us to overlook the impact that change has upon people. As managers, it might be easier for us to have only employees who can "take it on the chin," but it is hardly realistic. A manager skilled in change acknowledges the range of reactions and works with, not against, these feelings.

When preparing to discuss change with an individual, it is important for the manager to understand what the employee's reaction to negative and positive change will be. This way, the manager will not overreact when a normally good worker exhibits hostile or angry behavior. Anticipating the behavior allows one to manage the behavior rather than react to it. Let's look now at the individual's sequence of reactions when confronted with negative change.

INDIVIDUAL RESPONSE TO NEGATIVE CHANGE

It is one of the unfortunate aspects of organizational life that a manager must sometimes impose change on an individual knowing that it will have a negative impact. Of course, the manager should avoid doing so if at all possible. This is part of a manager's obligation in building humane organizations. Regrettably, unpleasantness cannot always be avoided, so the manager's obligation then becomes to manage the employee during this change with skill and tact. Most employees, when confronted with negative change, will go through five phases.

Shock: When employees are informed of change that will have a negative impact on their working life, the first reaction is shock. Unpleasant surprise has overtaken them. They will initially be unbelieving and will doubt what they have heard. The manager should be prepared to explain the situation several times and to respond to the employees' urgent request for the reasons.

Fear: Shock is rapidly replaced by fear. Depending upon the degree of threat, they will first of all fear a loss of pay, power, and status. Their basic security will be threatened. They also fear what others will think of them. If the change involves a transfer, which tends to be the most negative of change, employees may fear a loss of control over their own destiny. It is very possible that some staff members have been building a career in a certain area or need to retain a certain position in order to move onto another job. A transfer out of that position can mean that those years of work will be laid waste. Employees will also fear that they will be transferred to a place and position that they do not like. If the library has branches, they may also lose money and time through increased travel. They also will fear that they are losing the work group that may have surrounded them for years and may fear building new relationships.

INDIVIDUAL RESPONSE TO NEGATIVE CHANGE

Shock

Fear

Anger

Depression

Outcome

Integration   Alienation

The fear that employees experience is very unpredictable. As knowledge of the situation increases, different fears will emerge. Managers must never assume that they have a handle on the situation.

Anger: Before employees have fully articulated their fears, they will experience anger. Employees will demonstrate a "they can't do this to me" attitude and will speak widely and negatively about the person who has brought about the change. The most destruction to the organization comes about in this phase. Angry employees file grievances, everyone takes sides, and the credibility of management can be damaged. Worse, this anger and this event will be remembered for a long time, and managers can be reminded years later of their treatment of employees. The main difficulty with this phase is that, unlike shock, anger will surface and re-surface for an extended period of time, depending upon the employee's ability to adapt and the manager's skill.

Depression: Closely intertwined with anger is depression. It is often said that depression is anger turned inward. Once employees conclude that they are powerless over the situation and realize that they must make the change, they will become sad, unhappy, and listless. There will be a period of withdrawal as they adjust to the new situation. Sometimes this will translate into sullenness and will always be interspersed with anger and fear.

Outcome—Integration or Alienation: These are the two extreme outcomes on a spectrum of employees' responses to negative change. If employees can rescue themselves from non-productive behavior and the manager can help them, they can move to a state of integration. This state refers to an employee's ability to adjust fully to the change, to look forward to what benefits the change will offer, and to gain important knowledge about themselves and the organization.

The alternative is an alienated state. Here employees exhibit permanently indifferent or hostile behavior towards the library. This state is characterized by an "8 to 5" attitude, an absence of serious contribution, and a general suspicion of management.

Since this is a spectrum, people may exhibit varying degrees of positive or negative behavior. Moreover, managers should know that it is quite common for employees to start out in the alienated state and eventually move to an integrated state. Good employees will struggle against alienation if they feel the organization is intrinsically worthwhile. However, they will always retain the feeling of being "burned," and it is doubtful that the organization will ever have such power over them again.

Note that this sequence is surprisingly like a state of grief. This sequence can become particularly intense in the loss of a position or a favorite assignment. The key word here is "loss." Employees suffer a separation from something to which they were attached. A manager must not minimize, nor casually overlook, the depth and range of these feelings.

INDIVIDUAL RESPONSE TO POSITIVE CHANGE
Surprise
Trepidation
Acceptance

Individual Response to Positive Change: One of the true pleasures of being a manager is announcing a positive change to an employee. Often, this comes in the form of a promotion or a much-desired transfer or a special assignment. However, it can also be adequate funding for their new branch, monies for a special collection, or additional staff for their unit. The manager generally knows in advance that the information will be well-received. However, as with negative change, staff going through positive change also experience a series of feelings of which a manager needs to be aware. They may also exhibit changes in behavior that a manager must anticipate and observe.

Surprise: Some news of a positive change often precedes its official announcement, so an employee, upon hearing the good news, will experience surprise that is tempered by their previous knowledge. Staff taken completely by surprise may be a little puzzled as to why they did not know before. Too much surprise can also bring resentment, as people's need to be "in the know" will frequently supersede other emotions. However, all of this will quiet down quite rapidly as employees see the advantage of the change and begin to feel the pleasure that the benefits will bring.

Trepidation: The next stage is trepidation. This is, after all, a change. Employees may wonder if they are equal to the new assignment, can learn the new skill, or are ready for the level of responsibility. This phase will be colored by mild feelings of regret as these employees also face the loss of the known. They may be sad at leaving a work location or a work group if that is what the change calls for. Usually, negative aspects are not substantial enough to upset the benefits of the change in the employee's mind. A manager should be aware, however, that occasionally negative factors will offset the benefits of a change to an employee. It is not uncommon for employees to turn down new opportunities because they do not want to leave their work group or responsibilities. A manager in such a situation should explain the long-term benefits of the change and help the employee to see how advantageous the new situation is. Even then, some employees will still resist.

Acceptance: Employees typically move rapidly to the final stage, which is acceptance. They will prepare eagerly for what is about to come and will demonstrate positive vitality towards the change.

Be aware, however, that there will be mood swings even with positive change. Even though employees may feel generally positive towards their new position, they may also be depressed because of giving up the mastery they had in their former position or the social network that was there. We always feel loss when we say goodbye to the known. Any depression here should be mild, however, and should pass quickly. If a manager feels that an employee is having trouble accepting the new position, counseling the employee to find out what the problem is should help to move the employee along. What is a realistic timeframe? It depends upon the employee and the nature of the change. Do not be surprised if an employee who successfully held a high-level job for a period of years takes upwards of a year to adjust to a new position.

Notice that in both the positive and negative sequence, the length of the period of acceptance depends upon the nature of the change and the way that employees receive the information. It is important to get people through these feelings as rapidly as they allow in order to restore the organization and the staff to previous harmony.

In discussing the individual reaction to change, we have looked at the most dramatic sequence of feelings. Remember that people are unpredictable. What may seem to be a small change to a manager may bring out the full range of emotions in an employee. On the other hand, employees are constantly surprising managers with their cool acceptance of the most difficult problems.

STEP 2
Discuss the change

After preparing for the meeting, the next step is to discuss the change with the employee, explaining what has occurred and what the effects are likely to be. Allow the employee to ask as many questions as needed to understand about the change. If the change is negative, most employees will be insistent on knowing if the change is any reflection upon them. If it is, say so, although that fact should have been brought out much earlier in counseling sessions with the employee.

It helps for the employee to understand that sometimes the manager may have had no alternative. It was the employee's misfortune to be in the wrong place at the wrong time. While there is little excuse for an organization that does not take care of its staff, it is useful for the employee to understand all about the change and try to see it from another viewpoint.

In a negative change, try to explain the sequence of reactions that the employee will experience. Of course, if the manager senses that an employee will interpret such a discussion as patronizing, do not proceed. Being patronizing will only aggravate the situation.

The manager must be careful to not be emotional during the meeting, even if the employee is confrontational. If the manager becomes emotional or nervous, the chances of a successful interaction are reduced.

In negative change, most employees will attempt to negotiate to make the change more palatable. Of course, if there is room to accommodate the employee's feelings, do so, but do not change the decision or be defensive about it. Remember who is in charge.

Be honest with the employee. If a change is tough, there is no use pretending that it is easier than it is. In addition, listen closely to what the employee has to say. The employee's reaction is vital information to the manager who must monitor the employee's performance.

STEP 3
Keep the channels of communication open

After the initial discussion, the manager must keep the channels of communication open. The key to success in managing employees in change is constant communication.

In positive change, of course, such communication will be a pleasure. The manager and the employee can enjoy discussing the change and the beneficial effects it will bring.

An employee in negative change is another matter. However, it is even more important that communication stay open. Initially, the employee will wish to speak to the manager frequently. As time wears on, the employee will think of different things and will need to clarify some points with the manager. Be available. It is better for the employee to speak to the manager than to the union.

If a manager closes off from an employee at this time, negative reaction to change will only deepen and alienation will surely result.

In one aspect of communication, however, the manager should remain silent. When a negative change has occurred to an employee, it is a subject of considerable gossip for several weeks. While the manager needs to make the necessary announcements about the change, it is better to minimize to others what has happened. This helps the employee involved save face if need be and not remain a constant subject of conversation. The manager's role is to settle the problem down as soon as possible and refrain from unnecessary conversation on the topic.

One of the hardest aspects of managing a person in negative change is the very real difficulty the employee has in dealing with the manager afterwards. Usually, that manager becomes an object of dislike and will be unable to help the employee.

STEP 4
Monitor performance

A good manager should carefully track an employee who is experiencing change. This is not a matter to be taken lightly, nor should employees be left alone to work out their own feelings. This is a matter between supervisor and employee, and it is up to the organization to provide whatever assistance it can. Many times, particularly in negative change, a manager will feel powerless against the range of emotions exhibited. Even if an employee rejects help, a manager must still take an active role with that person.

Even if the manager is confident of the employee's performance, it is a good idea to regularly monitor how well the person is doing. Visits to the branch or department as well as regular meetings should provide the knowledge necessary to gauge performance. Setting some goals early on also helps the manager to see if the employee is able to carry out the goals as expected.

The manager should remember that the accomplishment of tasks is not the only measure of performance. How the employee is adjusting to the change is also an indication of how well the employee is doing. Does the employee have the mental discipline to cope with change? Can the employee disengage from a negative event in the past and deal with the future? Is the employee able to curb any destructive or angry behavior for the good of the organization? These types of questions, and their answers, reveal the employee's true performance.

Be particularly alert to one aspect of this. Employees in negative change frequently allay anxiety by talking compulsively about the change. If at all possible, the manager should encourage the employee not to become a victim of the change. Employees unable to handle change well may damage their future in the organization by demonstrating aberrant behavior. As much as possible, the employee must make the change a growth experience.

It is said that it is not what happens to people but how they react to it that counts. When the employees are ready, help them to look for the positive and not react to negative aspects more than is necessary. Employees soon come to regret their loss of pride and self-esteem.

Additionally, the manager must take some responsibility for the employee's performance by providing adequate support.

Make sure that employees have all the resources needed to adjust to the changes. If a transfer is involved, make sure all necessary training is provided. It is very common to tell employees that they are to report to such and such a position without offering orientation or training. No employee should be left to learn a new job alone. An employee struggling to learn a new assignment can experience unnecessary difficulty and become resentful.

The physical comfort of the employee should be considered. How many times do employees report to a new office with shabby paint, no drapes, no supplies, and no file case? Everyone remembers the uncomfortable feeling of an unprepared office. A manager should be conscientious in providing a welcoming environment. Obviously, if the situation is positive and the circumstances warrant it, then luncheons, announcements, or formal ceremonies are most appropriate. Such niceties make the employee feel welcome and proud. All of this will affirm the positive nature of the change in the employee's mind.

Employees in negative change should still feel welcome in their new position or assignment.

Employees may also need help in pacing themselves in their new assignment. This is a stressful time, and no one should be overloaded in such a period.

CONCLUSION

The obligation to manage employees in change is a serious one. Nothing will upset an employee more than a manager who appears indifferent to or unaware of the impact of change. The manager should work with the employee until the new process, system, or position is accepted. Most problems can be prevented by proper management at the beginning.

Managers should also evaluate their own performance. How well did they do? What could have been done differently? Managers should review how well each step was handled so that the next time—and there will be a next time—the process goes even more smoothly.

QUICK CHECK

STEP 1
Prepare for the meeting

A. Was the time and place selected?
B. Was the location selected?
C. Did the manager anticipate?

STEP 2
Discuss the change

A. Does the employee understand about the change?
B. Does the employee know what will happen?
C. Did the manager stay in control of the meeting?

STEP 3
Keep the channels of communications open

A. Is the manager available to the employee?
B. Has the manager clarified the employee's questions?

STEP 4
Monitor performance

A. Did the manager set goals with the employee?
B. Have regular meetings been set up?
C. Is the employee's behavior constructive or destructive?

7 CONTROLLING RESISTANCE

STEP 1
Identify the techniques of resistance

STEP 2
Analyze the source of resistance

STEP 3
Counteract resistance

When it comes to change, most managers find their Waterloo in employee resistance. For a manager, enthusiastic about a project, it is disheartening to struggle for the acceptance of an idea, let alone its implementation. All employees will resist change at some point. Unless the employees communicate their feelings, it will be up to the manager to fathom the reasons for resistance.

One of the hardest things for a manager to face is that even if change was properly communicated to the employee, resistance may still occur. When change is underway, the manager must be constantly alert to employee resistance. Once resistance has been noticed, the manager must understand the source of the resistance and move quickly to counteract it. If it becomes deeply embedded in the organization, it will be almost impossible to gather the support necessary for successful change. In controlling resistance, follow these three steps.

STEP 1
Identify the techniques of resistance

Resistance will manifest itself in a surprising variety of ways. Some will be covert, some very obvious, some will take longer to detect than others. Watch for the first signs. Let's look now at some of the techniques that employees will use to resist change.

Work slowdown: Rather than confronting managers directly, sometimes employees will use passive-aggressive behavior in the form of work slow-downs. While not always immediately obvious, this is very deadly. It is also very difficult for employees to sustain and management to tolerate.

Union action: Sometimes employees will go directly to the union, particularly if the change affects salary or working conditions. Union involvement in change will slow down the change process dramatically and may alter it so significantly that management will no longer be interested.

Gossip: Gossip is one of the most common ways to show resistance. It may seem harmless but, if malicious, can give a project or the people involved a bad reputation and thereby destroy the staff's confidence in the change. Gossip is a form of sabotage.

Setting up alternate systems: A prevalent way of displaying lack of confidence in the change is to set up alternate systems or to simply continue working in the old way. It is very common to have a new system and an old system exist side by side. For example, how many libraries found it hard to phase out the card catalog even though the automated catalog was fully functional? Alternate systems should be identified and discarded.

Refusal to learn new task: Resistance will also be manifested in the refusal to learn the new task. After all, if employees do not know how to do it, they cannot be expected to work with it.

Giving surface support: Sometimes resistance will be covert. People who are wary of speaking honestly, for whatever reason, may appear supportive but in reality not be. They will attend to the change in only the most perfunctory ways. This very subtle form of resistance will occur with people who do not want to defy the manager but are having major trouble supporting the change. Managers need to be careful of staff who give maximum enthusiasm but minimum compliance.

Dragging out the work: Dragged-out work in committee and missed deadlines are symptoms that people are resisting change. Once again, though overt support is given, the staff have not committed fully to the project.

Providing inadequate resources: This is the weapon of a supervisor resisting change. Without adequate resources, no change can take place. There will always be good excuses why resources should be anywhere except with the change.

Giving mixed messages: This also is the tool of a supervisor resisting change. Employees are quick to read these cues, and if they see supervisors giving an idea short shrift, they will too.

Notice that these are all pathological responses to change in the organization. A staff member who has problems with change should communicate those problems to the managers. Employees who are subverting the organization's goals lack confidence in themselves and in their work or do not have a good relationship with the managers.

STEP 2
Analyze the source of resistance

Once the techniques have been identified, the manager must look at why employees are resisting change. Let's look now at the causes of resistance.

Force of habit: The first of these is force of habit—people's need for stability and established patterns. Change reminds people that the unknown is all around them. Even the most adventurous amongst us still likes the familiar. Overcoming the fear of the unknown, and the rigidness of established patterns, is one of the challenging tasks in the management of change.

Fear of loss: Change can also bring loss. The loss of power, status, pay, work groups, job location, favorite assignments, position, control of destiny, and support groups are just some of the array of losses that employees may feel. These must be offset by considerable benefits in order to interest staff in change.

Insecurity: Change can create a feeling of insecurity. Employees accustomed to competence and mastery over their jobs might be faced with a period of learning during which they may feel foolish or stupid. Insecurity travels with the fear of failure. Employees will be wondering what will become of them if they cannot master the new task.

Ignorance: Sometimes ignorance causes resistance to change. Employees may simply lack the information to persuade them that the idea is a good one. Or they may have misinformation. The staff may be harboring some assumptions about the idea that persuade them that the change is a bad one.

Laziness: Laziness is also a factor. Major change requires major effort, and some employees may feel that the benefits do not warrant all the work.

No confidence in management: Employees may resist change because they have no confidence in the manager. There are two reasons for a lack of confidence: either the manager is not trustworthy, or the staff is predisposed to cynicism about management. A good manager may suffer from staff members' negative experiences with change in the past.

Excessive workload: Resistance may also be built up by an excess of work or stress. If the organization is already on overload, the staff is unlikely to welcome additional tasks.

Peer pressure: Sometimes peer pressure will cause people to resist the change. Since most employees' reality is shaped by their co-workers, it is difficult for a manager to overcome what has been said by fellow workers.

Feeling threatened: Employees, as well as managers not involved in the change, will resist change because they see resources needed for their own pet projects allocated for the change. Such an allocation of resources may threaten a task that they have been developing for an extended period of time.

Poorly managed project: Staff will resist change when they feel that the project is disorganized, poorly thought-out, and subject to bad decision-making. Most library staff is very well-educated. They respect organization and logic.

Discounting of staff: When staff attempt to participate in change and their opinions are disregarded, they feel discounted by management. As a result of this, they become uninterested or indifferent to the change.

Wasted work: If staff has been working hard on the project but decisions and goals keep shifting, their work is no longer relevant. This results in wasted effort. Staff will tolerate this once in a while, but if enough work is wasted, they will soon go on to things that are more productive.

Burnout: Finally, employees will resist change because they are alienated, unmotivated, or just plain tired. Burnout means that a person has nothing more to give. Change can only live in a creative, vital workplace. If there is enough burnout in the staff, change will not be able to thrive.

A manager needs to understand the motivation behind resisting change. Resistance always has a cause that can be identified. Frequently, the cause can be observed or inferred from behavior and communication. As often as not, employees will tell the manager what the problem is. This demonstrates the value of an open organization as it saves managers both time and mistakes in interpreting employee reactions.

STEP 3
Counteract resistance

Someone who is managing change effectively will anticipate resistance. A manager should be strategic about handling resistance as soon as it manifests itself. The following are techniques for managing resistance.

Create a safety net: If people fear the unknown, give them all the security that is needed through training, meetings, and information. It takes people a while to grow accustomed to change. The more familiar people become with the idea and what is involved, the more confident they will be about what is to come.

Manage the change well: Regardless of what management books hit the bestseller list, there is no substitute for sound management practices and a well-organized, well-considered approach to work. Employees will respond to the quality of the work and to the leadership demonstrated.

Be an example: A manager who is positive, assertive, and over-flowing with confidence about the success of the change and the ability of the organization to deal with it will set an example for the staff. While privately a manager may sometimes feel doubtful, those feelings should not be paraded in public. A manager should be a role model for the staff.

Make the resistors part of the project: If done with enough skill and with good employees, a manager can successfully urge people who are resistant into the project. This involvement may eliminate their resistance as they become more and more a part of the project. Of course, the manager needs to be careful or the project will be changed significantly or stalemated by resistors playing a key role.

Use peer pressure: If only a part of the unit affected is resisting change, a manager might consider using peer pressure. If the employees who are enthusiastic about the project sense that it could be stopped by the resistance, they might bring pressure to bear to get the resistors to give way. If the manager has the confidence of the supportive employees, some discussion might be had as to how to turn the others around. Be careful, however, that this does not backfire.

Discipline: Employees who resist all the efforts and charm of management may require more assertive action. If everything has been attempted and much is at stake, employees should be counseled and warned about their behavior. This is a last resort; more resistance may occur as a result of discipline.

Be honest: Even if employees disagree with the manager about change, there will be less resistance if the manager has a reputation for honesty. At least the employees will know that management is not attempting to trick them.

Communicate: Once again, let's emphasize the value of communication. Managers should speak often and frankly about the change. Staff should be asked to respond and should feel free to speak up even without being invited. Good communication is vital to the success of change.

The manager should be aware that techniques for counteracting resistance may be applied again and again to the same situation. Resistance, particularly resistance that has become deeply rooted in the organization, may emerge repeatedly from the same or from different people. The manager should apply constant pressure to overcome resistance.

CONCLUSION

Every manager should know that resistance can occur at any time in the change process, although it appears with most force when the project is fairly well along. A manager must be astute in identifying who the resistors are, how they are manifesting resistance, and what their reasons are for resistance. Once this is known, some techniques can be utilized to counteract resistance.

Consider also how much a manager is responsible for staff feelings about change. Unfortunately, after everything has been done, a manager still cannot abdicate the responsibility of working it through. To leave a staff member alienated is not acceptable. Everything must be done to get the staff behind the change.

One final note: a manager controlling resistance is in a conflict situation. The manager may find this both heartbreaking and lonely. Expect no compassion from staff. They will be very hard on any manager who seeks to control their resistance.

What if there is no resistance to negative change? Then either the change does not have the power that managers thought or the workers are apathetic.

QUICK CHECK

STEP 1
Identify the techniques of resistance

A. Is the staff on a work slowdown?
B. Has the staff approached the union?
C. Is there excessive gossip occurring?
D. Have alternative systems been set up?
E. Has staff refused to learn the new task?
F. Has only surface support been given?
G. Is the work being dragged out?
H. Have inadequate resources been provided?

STEP 2
Analyze the source of resistance

A. Is the staff caught in force of habit?
B. Does the staff fear a loss?
C. Is staff insecure?
D. Is the staff ignorant of the change?
E. Is the staff lazy?
F. Does the staff have confidence in management?
G. Does the staff have an excessive workload?
H. Has the staff succumbed to peer pressure?
I. Does the staff feel threatened?
J. Is the project poorly managed?
K. Has staff been discounted?
L. Is there wasted work?
M. Is the staff burned-out?

STEP 3
Counteract resistance

A. Was a safety net created?
B. Was the change managed well?
C. Were the managers a good example?
D. Were the resistors assigned to work on the change?
E. Was peer pressure used?
F. Were employees disciplined?
G. Was the manager honest?
H. Is there good communication?

IMPLEMENTING

Implementation is the process that moves the organization from the current state to the desired state. It is the phase in which the concepts and the plan for change are brought into being. During implementation, the design of the change must be integrated into the organization's existing structure and processes.

Implementation calls for great attention to detail as well as a steady and thorough approach. To achieve successful implementation, follow these seven steps.

STEP 1
Appoint a transition manager

STEP 2
Choose the right timing

STEP 3
Formally introduce the change

STEP 4
Pilot the change

STEP 5
Avoid change disintegration

STEP 6
Follow-through with the change

STEP 7
Release the trappings of change

STEP 1
Appoint a transition manager

While managers are always ultimately responsible for any occurrence in the organization, someone else may need to be in charge of the project's day-to-day operations. This is particularly true in change of any magnitude or difficulty. It is a common practice in libraries to assign projects to staff already overloaded with work. When a project is substantial and complex, it requires a great deal of attention. If it is just one of too many responsibilities shouldered by a staff member, it will never receive the care it deserves. The result, of course, will be an erosion in the quality of the project.

Consider appointing a transition manager who will take responsibility for the successful implementation of the project. This person should have as much authority as possible and should act in the place of the manager. A transition manager can be very helpful, particularly in technological change. The library can hire outside experts to develop systems if such people are not available in-house. The transition manager's job is to handle the people affected by the change, ready the organization to receive the technological change, and handle much of the business side of technological development such as securing budgets and managing contracts. Frequently, when libraries develop new automated systems, the person who handles the technological aspects is also expected to manage the overall change and deal with the upset emotions of the staff. This range of skills is not common. If your library has a manager with all these qualities, by all means appoint that person. Otherwise, look for a transition manager who has good management and good people skills and who will be able to see a project through to successful conclusion.

STEP 2
Choose the right timing

The timeline for the project should have been developed in the planning phase. That timeline should illustrate the time necessary between each critical event in the change. The timing that we consider in implementation is different. Let's look at this in more detail.

The best of times for implementation to occur is when very few other changes have happened, when the budget is sound, and when there are no other major projects. Although such control might not be possible, the manager must avoid overloading the organization with too many changes or large projects at once.

If the timing is poor, people will not accept change no matter how valuable the concept may be. It is surprising how many managers will introduce major change when there are too many staff vacancies or there have been unwilling transfers, work actions, negotiations, budget cuts, severe disagreements, or other major assignments. This attention to task and non-attention to people can spoil the beneficial effects of the change and certainly expose the managers' competency to harsh criticism.

The manager should try to anticipate events that will affect the workload of the library and so impact on the quality of the change. This is not as difficult as it sounds since such items as budgets, reports, ordering, and grants are often cyclical. The manager may also want to consider what other projects can be placed on hold to give the change a good chance to succeed.

Experienced managers will ask what happens when the timeline and the timing were properly selected but there is an uncontrollable event that forces the pace of implementation to accelerate greatly? If this is inevitable, and it does happen with some frequency, look at these several techniques for dealing with hasty change.

Stick to the process: The process, the phases of change that we have discussed, should be adhered to. The phases are based on logic, so a manager should not skip around or eliminate any. It is very tempting when under pressure to race ahead and make decisions without adequately considering the consequences. Obviously, there will not be the time for formalities, excessive documentation, or large committee gatherings, but the sequence of change should still remain.

Be positive: When change has to be implemented in a hurry, it usually is the result of a negative circumstance. Although the managers might be angry and upset at the threat to the organization, make sure that they all maintain a positive outlook.

Do not permit angry managers to be doomsday machines. The situation may be the most awful to have ever hit the library, but panicking and upsetting the staff won't help. It is only a temporary gratification. Such times call for cool heads and a steady hand.

Take time for people: In hasty change, it is easy to attend to task and to forget about people. This would be a mistake. You should explain the situation to the staff so resentment will not build up over the sudden or excessive workload. In such periods, managers want staff to rally around them in order to achieve the goals.

Be consistent: An organization under pressure is not the place for managers to act out of character. While there may not be time for the usual niceties, remain consistent in management style. If the manager has a history of being participative, allow staff to have as much input on the changes as possible. Stepping out of character at this time will only confuse the situation and damage your relationship with other people in the future.

Be comfortable changing decisions: Decisions made under pressure are not always good decisions. In addition, pressurized situations often change rapidly, putting the organization or the problem into a different framework. Be comfortable altering a decision based on new information. Of course, explain the change but do not feel wedded to decisions made in haste.

STEP 3
Formally introduce the change

Even though the manager has been completely open about the change, always give the change some type of formal introduction. This makes the change clear to people and offsets resentment that staff may have about being left out of vital information. This is particularly critical in libraries where the staff feels a very strong need to know.

The formality or preparation of the introduction depends upon the magnitude of the change. Consider whether the change can be announced in a memo or whether it requires a meeting with staff.

If those employees most affected by the change are not yet aware of it, tell them first. Never, never let people learn about the disposition of their work from anyone but their supervisor. As we have discussed, if the news will be negative, the manager needs to set up a small, closed session for the affected employees. All details about the change should be available to the affected staff members at that time, and the manager should try to handle their problems during the meeting. Since the manager already knows what the sequence of emotions will be, it is better to deal with the difficulties head on than have negative emotions spill over into the organization. Realize that, within a few hours of the meeting, the rest of the staff will know all the circumstances of the change. In spite of that, allow a little time before a general meeting is called to allow the affected staff time to resume their self-control.

If a general meeting is called to announce and to discuss the change, think through in advance who needs to be there and who can be informed instead by their supervisor. If the change might provoke hostile reactions, consider a smaller group. That way, their problems can receive more attention, and people will not bounce reactions off each other as much. If the manager has held a smaller meeting previously, be prepared for the fact that the affected staff may be organized to give the manager a difficult time. If it looks as if a general meeting might get out of hand, delay it until emotions cool down and people have a chance to adjust to the change. It will do the manager no good to walk into the lion's den, and the change will be badly damaged by so negative a beginning.

As change is introduced to the staff, be sure to have its benefits in mind and do not gloss over any problem areas. Any casualness at this point will damage the project and prevent people from taking it seriously.

If the change has been highly confidential, remember that the manager will be dealing with people's initial surprise and, possibly, resentment. Let people blow off steam; it is better to have such emotions in the open.

It may also be possible to have a person other than the manager introduce the change. This may be advisable if the staff is upset with the manager over a previous occurrence and, therefore, not as receptive. The person representing the change is crucial. The substitute should be well-respected and influential. A person who has no credibility cannot give the change any credibility.

A manager should be both visible and accessible throughout the implementation process. An informal walk through the units or departments can clear up a lot of problems. In times of stress, information may be the only help that can be given, and the primary source of information is the manager. Most managers will be surprised at what problems can be solved on the spot by a quick discussion with staff.

STEP 4
Pilot the change

Do not hesitate to pilot parts of the change before a full implementation. A mock run, if that is possible, or a gradual phasing in, with interim procedures, can supply a lot of knowledge about the change. If the change promises to be rocky, it is better to expose only a small part of the organization to problems rather than the total organization. Do not pilot the change haphazardly, however. In their eagerness to see a good idea carried out, managers will often pilot the change before the full design is completed. While it is acceptable to pilot the change to see if the design works or to pilot parts of it during implementation, do not pilot it ahead of conceptualization or planning. This piecemeal approach will cause more confusion.

In addition, since the pilot will tend to become part of the organization, it should be as close to the final design as possible.

Be aware, also, that the pilot is a public relations device for the change. If the pilot works well, people will assume the full change will also. If it does not, people will assume the change was a poor idea. If the pilot has problems, continue to be positive about the change and sincere about working out the problems. If staff members see a positive, assertive approach, they will be secure in their belief that the project is being managed properly.

STEP 5
Avoid change disintegration

The disintegration of change—the fraying, erosion, and eventual end of the project—is the foremost problem confronting the manager who is managing change. The spectre of disintegration hovers over any change, but particularly change of great magnitude or difficulty. Usually, the change has disintegrated before the manager realizes the extent of the problem. At this point, most managers attempt to intervene to rescue the project only to discover that the change has disintegrated beyond recovery. Sometimes, managers do not know that the change has disintegrated. In this situation, the manager may be pushing hard for the change, and the staff, attempting to comply with the manager's wishes, will keep up a good appearance about the project. Unfortunately, the staff will be deeply angry about being placed in such a predicament and will in all likelihood make the manager the target of anger.

The key to offsetting the possibility of disintegration is identifying the problem early enough to control the damage. Fortunately, the warning signs are obvious. For example, look at this list for cues to disintegrating change:

> Frustration in the planning group.
> Meetings that have an angry quality.
> No progress even if people have agreed on decisions.
> Resignation from the task force, pleading other responsibilities.
> Formation of sub-groups.
> Serious hallway conversations.

Why does change disintegrate? Fear, confusion, stress, and fatigue appear to be the causes. Why should these emotions be awakened? Let's look at the reasons.

Loss of purpose: Loss of purpose is one of the most common reasons for change disintegration. Suddenly the group does not know where it is going or why. They have become so lost in the process that the purpose is blurred. There are two primary causes for this. First, the change might be too large for the group to handle. There is only so much data that the human mind can handle at once. Over time, people can sort out almost anything, but if a short deadline is combined with massive change, the staff may well be unable to analyze the complexity and break it into manageable units. Fatigue will definitely play a role here, as will frustration.

Second, a leader or manager may have unconsciously introduced new goals into the project. The planning group, equally unconsciously, will accept the new goals and throw the project off-base. Since all of the planning was dependent upon achieving the goals, the entire process will be skewed. It is imperative that a manager hold a true course and take on realistic projects.

Glossing over problems: Another major cause of change disintegration is the glossing over of problems by the manager or the planning group. If problems are conscientiously brought forward, they must be responded to with equal conscientiousness. Managers will usually gloss over problems when they have made up their minds on the project before all the information is in. Ignoring or minimizing problems might speed the change along, but will eventually be destructive to it. This glossing over of problems is profoundly frustrating to the staff and eventually forces them to opt out of the process.

Introduction of new facts: New facts coming to light midway through the project also create problems. Sometimes this is unavoidable; sometimes it is a result of carelessness in the early stages of managing change. Although many new facts can be accommodated, occasionally the new information will damage the project. This problem should alert the manager to the possibility of other underlying forces. Consider whether the project was dealt with piece-meal when it deserved a broader perspective. Tackling a problem on too narrow a basis means that one has not considered the organization as a whole.

Sometimes the new elements that must be dealt with are emerging values and feelings of the group undergoing change. This may not be known before the change is underway, as it is the threat of change that brings these values and feelings to the surface. Such elements may intrude upon the change process and negate the benefits of change.

Unanticipated pressures: Sometimes unanticipated pressures in the organization bring about disintegration. The change may have been well-timed and well-planned, but an unexpected event might upset the change. For example, a sudden budget loss could put an end to a new facility. A heavy turnover in staff might upset the planning for a circulation system. Managers need to know that it is not always their fault that change has disintegrated.

The scope and authority of the planning group: Failure to fully identify the scope and authority of the group can also cause the group to fray. A group that has less responsibility than anticipated will feel frustrated by a lack of decision-making authority. Eventually, its members will begin to see their work as peripheral. A group that has more responsibility than anticipated can also have problems because the leadership of the group may not have been set up for that level of responsibility. A group that lacks proper leadership will also lack proper direction and be frustrated. Make sure that the scope and authority of the planning group are clearly stated.

Project mismanagement: Probably nothing brings about change disintegration more than project mismanagement. In this situation, staff grows so frustrated with the problems that they permit the change to disintegrate.

Look down this list for signs of a mismanaged project:

There is no follow-through by managers when questions are asked.
Managers do not listen to recommendations.
Inadequate resources are provided.
Project is not well-organized.
Presence of equally major projects that always take precedence.
Inadequate staffing is provided.
Managers lack knowledge about the project.

When a project is not getting the attention of management, the employees follow suit. Be attentive to the management of the project.

STOPPING CHANGE DISINTEGRATION

When a manager sees the behavior of change disintegration in a group, it is best to stop the process and unravel the problem. An honest conversation with staff, who themselves may not understand what is happening, will usually put the project back onto track again. If the causes of disintegration are deep-seated, it may take several meetings to understand what went wrong. Sometimes the task force is having problems with the manager. If there has been enough openness in the organization, the staff may be able to broach this clearly. If not, look for signs such as people looking down, being silent, or being irritated during meetings. Unfortunately, it is asking a lot of managers to have enough self-awareness to know when they are the problem.

Once the cause of change disintegration has been identified and solved, the manager should consider speeding up or slowing down the process to give it a new feeling of vitality. Replacing one or two people who might have bitter feelings about the project is also a possibility. However, there are two dangers here. People who are bitter might affect the feelings of others about the change. It might be better for those people to remain and work out their approach to the project. The other danger is that new people will want to explore old territory, even as far back as early goal-setting. This will frustrate the others immensely and may bring about a second disintegration.

If a manager feels that a project is a likely candidate for change disintegration, then some consideration might be given earlier on to developing contingency plans. This will give the manager a safety net if plans fall through.

It is hard to face the reality that a promising change can disintegrate. Perhaps the central idea was weaker than supposed, or perhaps the motivation to change was not as strong as supposed. The manager must decide whether the change is disintegrating as a result of problems that can be solved or as a result of an inherent weakness in the plan. A realistic appraisal of events, and a little executive intuition, should indicate which of the two this is.

No manager should permit the project to simply disintegrate. Instead, the manager should loop back to the phase of deciding on change and abort the change.

Every manager must be aware that change can disintegrate at any time. It often happens in implementation because implementation forces the design of the change to confront the reality of the organization.

STEP 6
Follow-through with the change

It is surprising how much change is planned but never comes to pass. Unless there are very good reasons to stop the project, make sure that the change is implemented, on schedule and as promised. Follow-through is critical in implementation.

The best way to ensure that we follow-through with change is to program it with a series of meetings, assignments, and due dates. The project should not be allowed to lag. At every meeting, the problems and assignments should be reviewed and people should be held accountable for their responsibilities. In addition, as soon as one assignment is completed, give another. This will give the change the impetus needed to succeed.

Once people begin working on a project, a high level of activity will overcome normal, but not abnormal, resistance. Allow people to make minor changes and suggestions at this stage, particularly about their individual assignments. When people place their stamp on things, their commitment to the project will increase.

Once change has been decided upon, it should be implemented with speed and certainty. Change that drags on too long or whose implementation is haphazard or non-existent, makes victims of everyone in the organization and eventually becomes pointless and an object of ridicule.

Keeping people on track requires assertive management, but it is best to keep the energy and interest levels up.

STEP 7
Release the trappings of change

After the implementation phase is complete, let go of all the trappings of change. The transition manager and task force are disbanded and interim policies are replaced by completed policies and procedures. Also, a memo announcing the completion of the change should go out to all staff. From this point on, it should be business as usual. But remember two points. First, thank everyone who was involved with the project in person and in writing. The letter or memo should be personal, alluding to their unique contributions, and signed by the manager, not the manager's secretary. This is simple courtesy and good management. This letter should be placed in the employee's personnel file. Second, remember that no change is ever permanent. The manager has created an organization that may appear stable, but the truth is that the organization is always in motion, always undergoing change.

CONCLUSION

Implementation requires a full and deep-seated commitment to the project. It is easy to get caught up in the design phase and the pleasure of creativity, but it is a very different matter to deal with the nitty-gritty of implementation. It is in this phase that the change becomes a reality and people are confronted with the fact that now they must change.

A manager interested in a successful implementation must be attentive to sequence and timing and be sure to follow-through. Implementation is often a period of doubt, but if careful planning has taken place, the manager should implement the plan with confidence and look forward to evaluating the success of the work.

QUICK CHECK

STEP 1
Appoint a transition manager

A. Will a manager take charge of the change or will there be a transition manager?

STEP 2
Choose the right timing

A. Has the manager considered what else is occurring in the organization?
B. Will the change have to be implemented in haste?

STEP 3
Formally introduce the change

A. Will the manager introduce the change through a memo or meeting?
B. Has the manager first informed those affected by change?
C. Who will make the introduction of change?
D. Is the manager visible and accessible?

STEP 4
Pilot the change

A. Does the manager want to try out the change on a small part of the organization first?

STEP 5
Avoid change disintegration

A. Has there been a loss of purpose in the group?
B. Have problems been glossed over?
C. Were new facts introduced that upset the change?
D. Were there unanticipated pressures?
E. Was the scope and authority of the planning group fully defined?
F. Has the project been mismanaged?
G. Has the manager taken assertive action to stop the disintegration?
H. Should the project be aborted?

STEP 6
Follow-through with the change

A. Is everyone sticking to schedule?
B. Does everyone know their assignments?

STEP 7
Release the trappings of change

A. Are all policies and procedures in place?
B. Has everyone been thanked?

9 EVALUATING

The most neglected phase in the management of change is of evaluation. When the implementation is barely complete, the managers and the staff are off to a new project or catching up with work delayed because of the change. Unless a major problem occurs with the change, this phase will never intrude and will be easily forgotten. However, evaluation is as critical as any other phase because it tells the manager if the change did what it was supposed to do. If it did not, then the problems or the pressures that created the change will emerge again. In addition, the evaluation phase fosters learning; it is an opportunity to go back and see how we did. Having this type of awareness will greatly enhance the likelihood of successful change in the future. Follow these nine steps.

STEP 1
Choose the time for the evaluation

STEP 2
Appoint the evaluators

STEP 3
Re-examine the goals

STEP 4
Choose the method of evaluation

STEP 5
Identify the problems

STEP 6
Avoid roadblocks

STEP 7
Make needed adjustments

STEP 8
Review the change process

STEP 9
Share the information

STEP 1
Choose the time for the evaluation

There is no hard-and-fast rule for when to schedule the evaluation period. It depends completely on the project. A major change that was costly and difficult should be evaluated several times: right after completion, and at six-month or one-year intervals. In fact, if the change was very difficult, it can be evaluated regularly until everyone feels comfortable that it is working correctly. A minor change could be evaluated within a few weeks and then not again. Decide early when the evaluation of the project will occur and stick to that schedule. In addition, make sure that all the staff is aware of the time schedule for the evaluation. If they know, they can be more conscious of problems and ready to indicate those problems to the evaluators.

The only time that staff members should not be informed of the evaluation period is when they are to be observed without their knowledge. While managers should approach this type of evaluation with caution because it can be very threatening to the staff, such evaluations can produce considerable knowledge. Retail businesses and transportation industries, such as airlines, regularly use "shoppers" who, in the guise of customers, assess the staff's ability to deliver good service. If a manager wants to assess reference or circulation services, for example, such a shopper could be used without the staff's prior knowledge.

STEP 2
Appoint the evaluators

The appointment of staff to evaluate the change again depends upon the magnitude of the project. A minor change should require only one person who worked closely on the change. A major change might require a team of several so that all aspects can be considered.

When appointing the evaluators, be sure to have one person who was closely involved with it and one person who must deal with its results. For example, if a change was made in the catalog, the manager may want a reference librarian who is using the catalog to be part of the evaluation team. The reference librarian can speak from the point of view of a customer. Also it is better not to choose evaluators from the former planning group only because they have too great an interest in the project being completely successful. In addition, they are too close to it to see it with the objectivity and balance critical for a good evaluation.

On the other hand, do not choose someone who has no background in the change. An evaluation done by someone with inadequate knowledge will be superficial and naive. It is demeaning for staff members who are experts in an area to be evaluated by someone without proper credentials.

STEP 3
Re-examine the goals

All evaluations should be done within the framework of the original goals. The purpose of an evaluation is to see whether the organization accomplished what it said it would in the change process. To use a previous example, if the goal was to increase the book shelving speed from 50 books to 70 books per hour, then the evaluation should show whether the shelving speed is now 70 books per hour. The evaluators should re-examine the goals closely and have them firmly in mind in order to determine if they were met.

Evaluators should look to see not only if the goals were realized but also if the goals shifted. Large-scale change is particularly susceptible to shifting goals. Change can begin to take on a life of its own, and it is very easy to shift to goals that will suit the change rather than making sure that the change suits the goals. Change that no longer fulfills its original purpose should be aborted.

At this point, notice the value of goals that were quantified when originally set. It is easier to begin with the knowledge of what results we want to achieve. For example, say a manager wanted to improve the number of inter-library loans processed per hour. If the evaluators know precisely how many per hour constitute an improvement, they would not have to re-create or fabricate what they hope is an acceptable number for evaluation purposes. How do we know whether improvement has occurred if we do not have a base line from which to measure expected results?

STEP 4
Choose the method of evaluation

With the goals clearly in mind, the evaluators should choose the method of evaluation. The method should reflect what the goals are and what the change was about. For example, if there were complaints by patrons about reference service, it would do little good to survey the staff to see if service has improved. It is also futile to call randomly using the telephone book to ask the public's response to reference service. Obviously, it is the library's patrons that must be surveyed. The evaluators should take care to match the method of evaluation to the goals and to the change.

There are many methods of evaluation, some formal, some informal. Informal ones can consist of evaluators going into the area of the library where the change occurred and stopping to chat with staff and users about the change. People will often respond frankly to this type of communication. The manager and the evaluators should also consider discussing the change as part of a regular business meeting with other areas that need problem-solving. One-on-one conversation with the staff may also demonstrate how successful or unsuccessful the change is. People will relay negative information more readily in a private setting, particularly if they are assured of confidentiality.

A more formal review might consist of a meeting called specifically to discuss the change. All the affected staff and the planning staff should participate. More formal still would be questionnaires or surveys that guarantee anonymity. However, questionnaires can be perceived as additional work-load or yet one more study that will bear no fruit. Obviously, if there is only a small staff, questionnaires would be a little pretentious.

For a library that is extremely serious about an evaluation, consider using an outside resource such as a consultant or a marketing firm. Such people are experts in determining work flow or public opinion. Evaluations that require the latter are greatly assisted by companies that do public surveys routinely. In addition, if the evaluation calls for the staff to be observed without notice, an outside company is essential, since staff from inside the library would be recognized. Moreover, no staff member should be requested to spy on another. Make sure that the evaluation does not concentrate on the results of the product or task alone. Look also at the impact of the change on people. For example, change that involves a reclassification or restructuring of employees can often have a negative impact upon a few employees while benefiting the organization as a whole. Clearly, there is a problem if loyal and dedicated employees were victims of the change process. Look at all dimensions of the organization to determine the success of the change.

STEP 5
Identify the problems

Whatever the method of evaluation, it is essential to identify all the problems connected with the change. Evaluations must determine not only whether the goals were met, but also the reasons for goals not being met. For this, the evaluators and the manager must look deeply at the work flow, the change process, and at communication to see what problems have occurred and how they can be corrected. This is why honesty and openness in organizations is essential.

As we have already discussed, be aware that sometimes the stated problem is not the real problem. If the change is difficult and people are having a rough time adjusting, their emotions may cloud or confuse the issue. Good evaluators must probe to see what the real problems are. Only when the real problems are identified can the change begin to work.

Even if the evaluation shows that the goals were met, there can still be problems. The achievement of quantifiable objectives does not mean that the change does not need any further correction. It can be made that much better by eliminating as many difficulties as possible.

When identifying problems, remember to discuss the change with all the affected staff. Everyone's experience and perspective will be different enough to offer the evaluators good insight into the problems connected with the change. Discussion with everyone affected will also allow the evaluators to see the total impact of the change upon the organization. When attempting to identify all the problems, it sometimes becomes evident that not all the facts are yet available. This means then that the timing of the evaluation is off. First, determine if the missing information is critical. If it is, simply put the evaluation on hold until the pertinent facts are available. If the unavailable data is minor, continue with the evaluation and pick it up later. One word of caution. When talking with staff about problems, be sure to keep discussions positive. There is a difference between problem identification and "getting the goods."

STEP 6
Avoid roadblocks

While most evaluations move smoothly, the manager and the evaluators may encounter roadblocks that prevent a good evaluation. It is important to be alert to deterrents to the evaluation process. Let's discuss three of the most significant and frequent roadblocks.

The first is the tendency to whitewash unpleasant situations. In this case, staff, despite known problems, will cover up the difficulties and give the change a good evaluation. Generally, this happens when it is not in the staff's best interest to reveal the truth about the change because it casts doubts upon them or upon a popular colleague or supervisor. The staff feels that they derive more benefits from covering up the inadequacies of the change than from revealing the problems. Without close questioning or a deeper penetration of the subject, it is very easy for a whitewashed situation to go undetected for a long period of time. With a major change, it is impossible to repress the problems forever. By that time, of course, considerable damage will be done. A small change that is whitewashed might go on for a very long time until staff decides to speak out or new staff takes over.

The second roadblock to a good evaluation is the sabotaging of the project as a result of personal vendettas. In this instance, staff will blow the problems out of proportion and will snare an unsuspecting evaluator into believing that the change is foundering. There are many reasons for such behavior, including dislike of a manager, alienation in the organization, or an inability to adjust to change. The danger of this roadblock is that not only will it affect the evaluation but the reputation, and eventually the outcome, of the entire project.

The third roadblock occurs when the staff feels that the manager will only accept a certain response to the change. If the manager is too wedded to an ideology in spite of all facts, the staff will rightly assume that no contrary evidence will be considered. Managers should avoid dogma in the management of change. A dogmatic point of view frequently forces people in subordinate positions to surrender their own viewpoints.

What is the cure for these problems? Certainly, they are difficult to observe and even more difficult to correct. The manager and the evaluators must retain their own steady judgment and not be overly influenced by any one person unless that person has a proven record as an accurate observer of events. An evaluation that is done with sophistication and a strong analysis in an organization that welcomes plain speaking will offset such roadblocks.

STEP 7
Make needed adjustments

Wherever it is noted that the goals were not met or other problems occurred, the manager should move swiftly to make the needed adjustments. If the planning process has been done correctly, the adjustments should be minor. If there are major adjustments, it would be worthwhile to call the planning group together again to correct the situation. Make sure, however, that the adjustments do not create new problems.

It is possible in the course of this step to discover that a bad decision regarding the change had been made. Managers should not take this as an issue of pride. A manager's overriding concern must be the success of the organization. If new information comes to light that invalidates a decision, simply alter the decision. Why make the staff and the total organization suffer with a decision that is no longer viable? Of course, a manager does need to explain this new development to the staff.

Managers should not be concerned that the staff will interpret changing a decision as weakness unless the manager always alters decisions. In that case, the manager may want to seek help with decision-making skills.

STEP 8
Review the change process

Not only should the project be evaluated to see if the goals were met, but the process should also be evaluated. There is much to learn every time we undergo change and, to prevent repeating problems, it is very important to evaluate the process carefully. Of course, the process does not just refer to the sequence of action, but also to such areas as our ability to handle people in difficult situations, to negotiate politically sensitive problems, to work together as a group, and to problem-solve on a broad scale. Wherever a manager notices a problem in the process, records should be kept to avoid the pitfall next time.

In reviewing the change process, the manager should also evaluate the length of time the project took. Sometimes change that goes on too long is harmful to organizations. Some projects, such as the automation of circulation systems, are by their very nature long-standing, but staff understands that and can work on the various preliminary phases. Lengthy change becomes destructive when staff positions are in a long period of indecision and the staff must face the anxiety of not knowing what will become of them or their assignment. When change goes on too long, apathy and indifference set in. It literally weakens the stamina of the staff.

The honesty of the change process should also be evaluated. Managers should beware of using misinformation, or disinformation. If a manager can give only partial information, say so. If a decision has been made but is confidential, say so. A good manager does not take people by surprise and certainly does not permit staff to hold assumptions the manager knows to be untrue. Managing by hints and half-confidences is a form of manipulation. Managers caught out in this process will not be considered trustworthy by staff again.

Lastly, the change process should be evaluated to see if hidden goals influenced the change. Not infrequently, people will instigate or manipulate change to fulfill their personal agendas. If these people are powerful enough, there may be displacement of what should be the true goals of the change. Hopefully, such antics will be caught early in the change process. Let's look at some hidden goals as examples:

Creation of a power base: The creation of a power base is a necessary fact of life for survival in organizations. All people need influence in order to be able to do their jobs. Part of that influence comes from the status of their position and from the power of their personal network. However, to create or influence a change purely for the purposes of building an empire is harmful. The staff's professional lives and feelings and the health of the organization are not fair game for anyone.

Self-Aggrandizement: To bring about change in order to build oneself an enhanced reputation, perhaps on a state or national level, is a wrongful manipulation of the organization. People should be ambitious, but should never plunge the organization into change in order to improve their own marketability.

The Bandwagon: Librarians are constantly pressured by journals, conferences, and colleagues to stay in the forefront of new ideas. However, if other libraries are adopting certain methods or styles, that does not mean that it is the best approach for all libraries. Change should only be brought about by careful thought, not because everyone else is doing it.

Managers must look honestly to ascertain whether hidden goals such as these unduly influenced the change. If so, some adjustment may be needed, and certainly steps should be taken to control hidden goals in the future.

STEP 9
Share the information

Once the evaluation is complete, the information should be shared with staff and library executives or governing boards. This is a time for celebrating the success of the project. The information can be shared either in a memo or by meeting. Not only does this let staff know that the change is here to stay, but that the manager is committed to its ongoing success. Also if the change has any nationwide or statewide significance, the managers should consider writing about the change so that others may benefit.

Equally important is information about an unsuccessful change. Sharing of negative information requires a very open organization in which the people are not afraid to take risks or to be candid about mistakes. Obviously, such information is delicate; no one should be put on the spot and embarrassed about unsuccessful change. Instead, managers should encourage the type of organization that looks at itself with clarity and frankness. Everyone can learn from this experience.

CONCLUSION

There are many good reasons for change in an organization. And there are as many bad reasons to change. Change should only occur when it is of benefit to the organization or when it must accommodate an occurrence beyond its control. However, it should never have an aim other than its stated purpose. When change has a shaky or suspicious foundation, people lose faith in the process and in managers. In the long run, such change is destructive to the well-being of the organization. Evaluating helps us to understand if the change we chose was good for the organization. It acts as a control over non-productive impulses.

Evaluating calls for steady judgment and the ability to see into situations of many kinds. We are all guilty of constructing our own reality, but to evaluate well we must be able to see things as they are. This also means divesting ourselves of ego. After all, if a manager has spent months on a project, it is difficult to hear that it has not succeeded. Avoid close personal identification with the project. Remember that to manage means to have control of, not to be controlled by.

QUICK CHECK

STEP 1
Choose the time for the evaluation

A. Should the project be evaluated after one month, six months or a year?
B. Should the project be continually monitored?
C. Should the staff be informed?

STEP 2
Appoint the evaluators

A. Have people outside of the planning team also been appointed as evaluators?
B. Are both designers of the change and users of the change on the evaluation team?
C. Do the evaluators have a background in the change?

STEP 3
Re-examine the goals

A. Is the evaluation within the framework of the goals?
B. Have the goals shifted?

STEP 4
Choose the method of evaluation

A. Will the evaluation be formal? Informal?
B. Will consultants be used?
C. Did the evaluation concentrate on all aspects of the change?

STEP 5
Identify the problem

A. Is the stated problem the real problem?
B. Has all the affected staff been interviewed?
C. Were all the facts available?

STEP 6
Avoid roadblocks

A. Was the change whitewashed?
B. Has the change been sabotaged?
C. Has the manager been too dogmatic?

STEP 7
Make needed adjustments

A. Has the manager corrected all the problems?
B. If a bad decision was made, has the manager hesitated to reverse the decision?

STEP 8
Review the planning process

A. Has the sequence of actions been reviewed?
B. Were people handled well?
C. Was the project handled well politically?
D. Was the organization able to problem-solve on a broad scale?
E. Were there any hidden goals?

STEP 9
Share the information

A. Was everyone informed of the evaluation?
B. Was the conclusion of the project celebrated?

CONCLUSION

Managers begin to build for change long before it occurs. Change places a lot of stress on organizations and, when under stress, any organization will reveal its true nature. A library manifests in its daily business the style and philosophy of its managers. If the managers are open and honest with staff and public alike, then, in difficult situations, the library will continue these practices. If the staff is accustomed to a humanistic organization that emphasizes cooperation and support, then no change can dislodge values. Change will bring out the best or the worst in people, depending upon the foundation that already exists.

For the effective management of change, managers must begin with an ethical framework that creates a supportive, cooperative, and harmonious organization. Every person on the library staff should be committed to building an organization that is a decent place to work. Together, we design organizations. Together, we are responsible for their success.

Moreover, managers must have control over the process of change. An effective manager is one who shapes the destiny of the organization. Far-reaching thought, consideration of consequences, and strategic thinking are the skills of a manager implementing change. The logic of change must be penetrated and held fast; the dynamics of change must be understood and anticipated. Change must be managed with control and foresight.

Finally, managers must be sensitive to people. People are complex and fragile. Change awakens many feelings that a manager must acknowledge. Comfort, compassion, and direction must be exercised to manage people in change.

When managing change, then, plan carefully and wisely and follow closely the steps outlined in this book. Now, let's take one last look at some of the most important points to be kept in mind when managing change.

Make no false promises: Until the change has been tested and evaluated, a manager should avoid making sweeping statements about what the change will accomplish. Promises that salaries will be improved, morale will be heightened, or things will be better will haunt the manager if change takes a downward turn. Staff will accept what the manager says and will be both disappointed and cynical if it does not come to pass. Of course, this includes promises made about positions.

Be honest: Managers without credibility are not effective. A morass of half-truths, misinformation, and partial confidences will damage the success of any project. It is better to be straightforward, even if that means explaining that some confidential information has been withheld.

Be fair: Sometimes people get hurt in change. Most of the time it is avoidable, but there are times when it is not. If staff has to be laid off or transferred as a result of budget cuts, be as fair as possible. If these opportunities have been used to get rid of problem staff, manipulate positions, or play favorites, an already difficult situation will be worsened. Remaining staff will observe the situation and be wary of the manager.

Take a systems perspective: Change will often founder because the approach has been too narrow or piecemeal. Remember that every part of the organization affects every other part. Knowledge of the relationship between parts of the organization is known as the systems perspective. Take the systems perspective in the management of any change.

Have a good reputation before beginning: It is important for library managers to face up to how their library staff really feels about them. Managers are all capable of a little self-delusion. If the staff is not supportive of a manager, then that manager is not the person to lead the change. Staff compliance is not the same as staff support. Before embarking on major change, make sure that a base of support exists.

Acknowledge the incentives for change: Generally speaking, the lower in the hierarchy of an organization people are, the less their preoccupation with the overall welfare of the organizations. A manager must let people know how they personally will benefit from the change. A library manager should consider what the incentives are for people at all levels.

Watch the environment: Every library has an internal and external environment—both of which can have a major impact upon change. If the staff is angry and upset, major change will not be well-received. The same is true in the external environment. If patrons are angry over service, major change may upset them further. Make sure that the internal and external environment is smooth enough to handle change.

Don't make anyone number one: This applies even if the manager is number one. Managers usually achieve their positions because they are willing to take chances and to be in charge.

Occasionally, though, strategic management means not being in the hot seat. If one person is the focal point of change, that person will be the victim if the change goes wrong. Change is a group process.

Provide the skills and knowledge: The "sink or swim" approach to training has always been popular in libraries. However, it is better to provide people who are accepting new responsibilities with full orientation and training. Adults are accustomed to feeling competent. In a changing situation, there is a loss of skill and knowledge that makes people feel insecure. Good orientation and training can restore a person to feeling in control over their position and will enhance their productivity.

Provide materials and equipment: Tangible resources should be provided to ensure that people are able to do their jobs. Materials and equipment should be factored into the planning process.

Work at all levels: This point has two meanings. In order to ensure success, a manager needs to work at all the levels of hierarchy in the library. Every level affected by change should be secured, but so also should every level above needed for approval. A manager needs to have the support above as well as below.

In addition, a manager should pay attention to all the levels within a person. For example, people may be drawn to change because of its rationale, because of their feeling about the change, and by the better service that it provides. If the manager appeals to all these levels, the change will win a more universal acceptance.

Help employees to know their role: One thing that change will accomplish extremely well is to upset the roles and relationships of people. As people take on new assignments or are moved to new locations, they suffer a loss of knowledge about their roles at work. A manager must make sure that adequate orientation and training are provided so that staff members understand their new roles.

Cover all the bases: Unless the library is very unusual, there will always be a percentage of people who will have a vested interest in seeing change fail. Even those who support it may turn away if the change goes sour. However, if the manager has netted all the relevant personnel involved in the change to "own" the change, there will be a body of support to help pull it back together if it should fail. Change needs a large and firm base of support.

Consider the political realities: Since there are very few libraries that are not part of a public or corporate entity, the political reality must be taken into account. A manager may feel that a certain change is good for the library, but if the board, the vice-president, or the dean do not agree, it is futile to pursue the change. Take into consideration at all times the power of political realities.

INDEX

Dr. Susan C. Curzon is a Regional Administrator for the Los Angeles County Public Library. Her doctorate is in Public Administration from the University of Southern California. She is also a Visiting Lecturer at the University of California, Los Angeles, Graduate School of Library and Information Science.

Dr. Bill Katz is Professor at the School of Library and Information Science, State University of New York at Albany. He is the author of many distinguished works in library science.

Book design: Gloria Brown
Cover design: Gregory Apicella
Typography: Roberts/Churcher